AFRICA'S
BROKEN HEART

D1044045

Hugh McCullum

AFRICA'S BROKEN HEART

Congo – The Land the World Forgot

WCC Publications, Geneva

The views expressed in this book do not necessarily reflect those of the World Council of Churches.

Cover photo: John Lewis, Kairos, Canada
Voters compare the purple dye used to identify people who voted at Kami-tugu Polling Station in South Kivu province, DRC, July 29, 2006.

Cover design: Marie Arnaud Snakkers

ISBN 978-2-8254-1506-1

© 2006, WCC Publications, World Council of Churches
P.O. Box 2100, 150 route de Ferney
1211 Geneva 2, Switzerland

Website: http://www.wcc-coe.org

No. 115 in the Risk Book Series

Printed in France by Lussaud
This printer has a green label guaranteeing environmentally-friendly printing procedures.

Table of Contents

Map and description

Flag: Light blue with a large yellow five-pointed star in the centre and a columnar arrangement of six small yellow five-pointed stars along the hoist side.

Democratic Republic of Congo at a glance
- Population: 65 million (estimate, no census)
- Capital: Kinshasa
- Area: 2.5 million sq km
- Major languages: Lingala, Kiswahili, Kikingo and 220 lesser but distinct dialects, French for the elites
- Major religions: Roman Catholic, Protestant and independent churches, small numbers of Muslim
- Life expectancy: 42 years (men), 44 years (women)
- Main exports: diamonds, gold, copper, cobalt, coltan, timber, crude oil

Area:
Total: 2,345,410 sq km
Land: 2,267,600 sq km
Water: 77,810 sq km
Area – comparative: Slightly larger than Western Europe

Land boundaries
Total: 10,730 km bordering nine countries: Angola of which 225 km is the boundary of Angola's discontiguous Cabinda enclave, 2,511 km; Burundi, 233 km; Central African Republic, 1,577 km; Republic of the Congo (Brazzaville), 2,410 km; Rwanda, 217 km; Sudan, 628 km; Tanzania, 459 km; Uganda, 765 km; and Zambia 1,930 km.

Maritime boundary
Only access to the sea is at the delta of the Congo River through a narrow strip of land where the DRC has 37 km of the South Atlantic Ocean coastline.

Climate
Tropical; hot and humid in equatorial river basin; cooler and drier in southern highlands; cooler and wetter in eastern highlands.

Terrain

Vast central basin is a low-lying plateau; mountains in east; dense tropical rain forest in central river basin and eastern highlands.

Natural resources

Cobalt, copper, niobium-tantalum (coltan), petroleum, industrial and gem diamonds, gold, silver, zinc, manganese, tin, uranium, coal, hydropower, timber.

A land of great mythology

It is the great Congo River, the continent's second largest, which gives the country its name and has lodged, in Western consciousness at least, a kind of mythic place, symbol of the unknown, of the primitive, of dense jungles made a legend by the British explorer, Henry Morton Stanley who trekked his way inland from Zanzibar on the Indian Ocean to the upper Congo and then drifted down the river 1,736 km, in pirogues (dugout canoes) arriving on the Atlantic coast in 1877.

He named the river Livingstone after the British missionary he had found near Lake Tanganyika in an earlier adventure ("Dr Livingstone, I presume"). His is probably the most extraordinary, not to say outlandish, story of the colonial scramble for Africa. Stanley claimed to have "opened up" the Congo by demonstrating its navigability across almost half of Africa and tried to interest the British in colonizing the huge land. When they showed no interest, Stanley sold the idea to the maniacal King of Belgium, Leopold II who, in 1885, managed to gain as his personal fiefdom this private rubber plantation with Stanley, the great Christian explorer, as manager of the newly named Congo Free State.

Joseph Conrad *(Heart of Darkness)* and V.S. Naipaul *(A Bend in the River)* among many other writers were fascinated with the river, soon renamed the Congo, and contributed to its sense of drama and tragedy under Leopold. It was the home of the great apes, huge varieties of monkeys, lemurs, elephant, buffalo, wild pig, leopards. There was the mysterious okapi – part zebra, part giraffe and from which today's Radio Okapi run by MONUC (the French acronym for the UN peacekeeping mission in the DRC) as the only non-political broadcaster in the country leading up to the 2006 elections derives its name. Birds, snakes and endless miles of jungle, massive hardwoods, piercing the canopy upwards of 50 metres, and unknown inlets and creeks. The Congo River is vital to the continent, huge and primal, a highway, sometimes as wide as 14 km, and easily navigated from Kisangani to Kinshasa, with enough potential hydro-electricity to power all of Africa.

"Ascending the river is like travelling towards the early beginnings of the world," Conrad wrote, "when vegetation covered the earth and the great rivers were king. A road of empty water, grand silence, impenetrable forest. The air is hot, humid, heavy, languid…"

Floating everywhere are islands of hyacinths, millions and millions of clumps of green leaves and pink flowers, drifting down to the rapids where they are chopped up in the wild waters and taken out to sea. They were introduced to Congo by a Belgian missionary who thought they might purify the river near where he was based. Instead, they have choked the Congo basin with flowers. These are no longer European hyacinths, they have become tropical in their size and fecundity.

Look at the Congo River on the map. It stretches around the country almost 5,000km; like a giant half-extended claw winding north from Zambia, it crosses the equator near Kisangani, the heart of the continent, veering west through the densest jungle on earth. Then it dips below the equator again before cascading into the Atlantic over 32 huge cataracts. People who live in this wilderness, even today, are among the most isolated in Africa, for there are almost no roads and these are impassable much of the year. In the absence of roads it has always been the country's lifeline, its watershed covers over 1.5 million sq km and more than 14,000 km of navigable tributaries. For years, river traffic – barges, ships, tugs, ferries and pirogues – provided a high-way for business and communication. Today most of the boats lie immobilized, rusted hulks, some even used as float-ing apartment buildings.

Gazing across a bend in the vast Congo river towards Kin-shasa, a tarnished bronze Leopold sits imperiously on his horse, facing the city which once bore his name. The bearded monarch's statue stands on a hill under two mango trees, surrounded by other colonial monuments in a neg-lected museum in the overgrown grounds of a palace built by Congo's former dictator, Mobutu Sese Seko.

Nearby lies a toppled likeness of Henry Morton Stanley, who cajoled local chiefs into giving their land to Leopold and who named Congo's main city, Leopoldville, in his honour. The moustachioed Stanley brandishes his snapped baton in his left hand. His broken-off feet stand to attention next to him.

These reminders of DRC's blood-stained history were long hidden from Kinshasa's residents after Mobutu stashed them away in a warehouse in the early 1970s.

Foreword

Not even God is wise enough… Yoruba Proverb

The beginnings of this story lie far back in time but its cruel, heartless reverberations still resound today.

The first contact between Europeans and a major state in sub-Saharan Africa began most likely around the 1480s when Portuguese missionaries came to the central African Kingdom of Kongo, located at M'banza-Kongo on the edge of today's border between Angola and the Democratic Republic of Congo. The missionaries were warmly received even though they were the first whites the people had seen. As missionaries are wont to do, they set about trying to make converts and, because the king, or Mani Kongo, was interested in obtaining European goods – including firearms – he gave the proselytizers a free hand. It was a not a fair exchange for the Kongo people and a dire warning of things to come.

Mani Kongo struggled valiantly with the consequences of this fateful decision over the coming decades and fought with extraordinary honour to keep his kingdom's head above water against what quickly became a Portuguese deluge. But there was no way to escape it. Just nine years after the first missionaries arrived in Kongo, the soul-saving rationale for the Portuguese presence in central Africa mutated almost overnight into something quite different: a rush to sell as many Africans as possible into slavery for colonies in the new world, Brazil.

Soon, expeditions were mounted many hundreds of miles from the coast, sowing panic and chaos among the people who were thrust into deadly competition with one another, and indeed against Kongo, one of the greatest kingdoms of Africa, rivalling Great Zimbabwe. It covered 300,000 sq km and likely was founded in the 12th century.

But by 1512 the demand for slaves outstripped anything known to Kongo society and the king, Afonso I, a fervent convert to Catholicism who could read and write, fought and argued with the Pope, the Church, and the Portuguese as his once flourishing kingdom began to collapse, undermined by the draining away of the nation's people. By the 1530s nearly half a million had been shipped to the Americas along routes that became known as the paths of death. Afonso watched in growing despair as the threads that held the realm together came unstitched. He wrote to his Portuguese counterpart, King Joao III:

> Every day the traders are kidnapping our people – children of this country, sons of our nobles and vassals, even people of our own family. Corruption and depravity are so widespread that our land is entirely depopulated. It is our wish that you, the king of Portugal, know and act on our wish that we do not want this Kingdom of Kongo to be a place for the trade or transport of slaves.

The king of Portugal's reply was brutal and simple, the death knell for Afonso's kingdom. Kongo, he said, had nothing else to sell. By the end of the 16th century it was all over. By 1795 only 100 people lived in what had been the glorious M'banza Congo, in 22 huts scattered among the imposing but decaying ruins of Christian churches.

* * *

This early history of the Congo has been repeated so many times that some revert to Conrad's *Heart of Darkness* to describe it as the "black heart of Africa". Larger than Western Europe, it was appropriated by King Leopold II of Belgium at the 1884-85 Berlin Conference which kicked off the European scramble for Africa. Leopold said his appropriation was for humanitarian reasons but in his more candid moments described his newly acquired territory as "a rich African cake". He ran it brutally as his personal domain and the Congo became synonymous again with cruel and shameless get-rich-quick schemes. For ivory, hardwoods, rubber and later copper, cobalt and uranium, the country saw one European rush after another.

Through stealth and extraordinary deceit, the king of Belgium persuaded his mighty neighbours that his work in the Congo would be driven by strict Christian principles. "I do not wish to receive one franc back of all the money I have expended," he promised. What followed instead was, in truth, one of history's greatest rapes. By the time King

Leopold was forced to cede control of the Congo Free State to Belgium in 1908 some 10 million Congolese had been murdered or died of disease and malnutrition – the worst genocide in the history of the world – half of Congo's population. Farming was made a crime when Leopold needed labour for the rubber plantations and violators had their hands chopped off. Thousands, no millions, of ears were strung on branches outside the offices of Leopold's agents, as witness that people who failed to meet production quotas were done away with.

Yet Leopold himself never saw a drop of blood spilled on his personal ranch for he never once set foot in the country that was his own and so, by 1909 when he died at 74, he left a legacy of holocaust heaped upon holocaust. In 1908, he actually sold the Congo to Belgium for about 200 million francs and his kingdom assumed all debts. His atrocities went unanswered. There has never been any remorse in the West over the fallout from Europe's drive to dominate Africa. Indeed, even today, few have heard the grim facts of the world's worst holocaust. (Historian and author Adam Hothschild's *King Leopold's Ghost*, Houghton Mifflin, New York, 1999, is a gripping account of this evil.)

In 1910 the Congo became the Belgian Congo until 1960 when independence was granted. While the country's atrocities generally remain unknown and the legacy of 10 million deaths is horrible enough, the impact of Belgium's takeover of the Congo created a tragic example of governance, essentially teaching that authority confers the power to steal, to brutalize, to oppress and to murder, rape and pillage with impunity. And the practical corollary to this lesson was that the bigger the title, the bigger the theft.

***

Leopold called his property The Congo Free State, Mobutu called his property Zaire, and now it is the Democratic Republic of Congo (DRC).

By 2006 war, diseases, and the consequences of violence and neglect had left another 4.1 million dead, the worst genocide since Hitler's Jewish Holocaust of World War II, and still no one seemed to know or care. The pillaging continued. The looting of Africa's richest country by foreigners was as if Leopold's successors were trying to outdo him. No elections were held for more than 40 years. Nine countries invaded the Congo in the first five years of the 21st century.

I had been to the Congo several times briefly in the 1990s when millions of Hutu refugees, the genocidaires of Rwanda's 1994 holocaust, fled into Goma and Bukavu intent on using then-Zaire as a base for resuming their plan to kill all Rwandan Tutsis. It was a ghastly sight and plan.

Over the years, as I learned more of DRC's history and the rape, murder and pillage that continued after dictator Mobutu left and died in exile and the DRC was formed, I asked myself and others, why is nothing done? Why is Congo a huge black hole in the news media? Does no one care? Often it was a topic of discussion at the WCC headquarters and the inevitable question: Why don't you go and write the story? I took the challenge and went to cover Congo's first democratic election in 46 years on 30 July, 2006. I spent a month in the ravaged heart of Africa before and after the elections.

I have worked and lived in most parts of Africa for more than 20 years. This was the hardest assignment I have ever had; physically, emotionally and spiritually.

The day Congolese voted in 2006 was reminiscent of South Africa's first election in 1994, an event I also covered. Like South Africa, millions of people walked many kilometres to cast their ballots in a moving sign of their belief that a democratic election might end their desperation and misery. The international community had promised them. The world's news media of that Sunday and the next day were filled with pictures and stories, Congo was on page one for a change. The next day, Israel invaded Lebanon, and Congo was relegated once again to the world's indifference and ignorance and disappeared from sight in the international media.

How long, these 65 million people ask. How long will the world forget us as it has for centuries? How many more must die? How many more women must be raped and mutilated? How many children must die of starvation?

Will the world ever remember?

Whenever the West pays any attention to Africa, it is often to lampoon its leaders. How conveniently we forget how this tragic pattern was set in place, in Congo, as elsewhere by what British novelist and social justice activist, John le Carré called with appropriate scorn "the global architects, the globalization men, the political charm-sellers, and geopolitical alchemists who in the cold war years managed, collectively and individually, to persuade themselves – and us too, now and then – that with a secret tuck here, and a secret pull there, and an assassination somewhere else, and a destabilized economy or two, or three, they could not only save democracy from its defects but create a secret stability among the chaos."

This book is intended to help remedy our complaisant forgetfulness and our criminal hypocrisy. My aim is to remind those who should yearn to know more of Africa and especially the Congo to remember and stop turning their backs on the hideous legacy of carnage left to the people of the DRC. It is time for us all to act.

Hugh McCullum
November 2006

Prologue: 65 million people the world forgot

The Democratic Republic of the Congo (DRC) is a country the size of Western Europe, where a vicious war has raged over a decade and cost the lives of more than four million Congolese. Some wars last long after they end. Four years ago in 2002, a peace deal was signed by the many factions in the DRC that was supposed to end a war that drew armies from at least eight other countries and produced human devastation unrivalled since World War II. Competing militias inflicted appalling suffering on the civilian population, and no one in what passes for international political leadership today was able to stop it. This is Congo, and the reason for the conflict – control of essential minerals on which the modern developed world depends – is what makes our blindness to the horror doubly shaming. Hugh McCullum went to central Africa for the World Council of Churches to cover the Congo election in July and August 2006.

There is no sky as big and deep and dark as an African sky. I awoke early one morning to a soft humming noise. A mosquito, I thought, remembering the rip in the net over my cot and Aru's high incidence of malaria (one million or more people die every year in Africa from the preventable mosquito-borne illness). As I fumbled for a candle, the humming grew louder but still soft and undulating. Can't be that many mosquitoes. I went to the small glassless window. The sun was just touching the horizon. About 4.30 a.m. The sounds grew, my eyes adjusted. I could see and was hearing a huge crowd of people about 50 metres from my room. A long orderly queue as far as I could see in the early dawn light. Sort of eerie, was it something religious on this Sunday morning, July 30?

Suddenly my brain clicked in – election day – but the polls didn't open until 7 a.m. There were thousands lined up around the voting station near where I had been sleeping. Solemn, quiet, patient, hands clutching their voting papers. By the time the poll opened it seemed half the town was there.

Aru lies near the top of northeastern Congo's Ituri province, one of the most war-scarred provinces in the DRC where more than 200,000 people are still displaced, driven from their villages into squalid camps. Aru district is just a few kilometres from the Uganda border. It is a MONUC base serving 132 polling centres which add up to 555 polling stations, most of them in the bush. None has electricity, even in Aru, and most can only be reached by air. For days and long into the night white UN helicopters had roared across the town and out to the bush, delivering all the paraphernalia needed for a national election in a country where there are no paved roads and the tracks through the bush that pass for roads are axle-breaking.

The election stories were endless and amazing. Two skinny, bent grandmothers set out on Saturday to walk 35 kms to the polling station and then, having voted for the first time in their lives, turned and walked back home through the bush. They were dressed as for a feast: "We have voted, now everything will be all right. No more violence, we will be safe."

Henriette Katuku Kishala, a nurse in a hospital built by the Belgians in 1926, which has no electricity, and sometimes does surgery by candlelight and kerosene lamp, said the elections would end the suffering. "It will make things change because we must have change, we have suffered too much."

In Ituri's capital, Bunia, a bashed-up city of unknown numbers, the main MONUC centre for the northeast, the blue berets from a couple of dozen or more countries are exhausted, dirty, dark circles under their eyes, but they laugh and dance and act as if they had voted themselves. "We did it, we did it," says a Pakistani corporal with huge handlebar moustaches. "We've been fighting here for months, lots got killed. Today, nothing. People walked for days, old people, crippled people, pregnant women, kids, everyone walked for miles and miles. Do you do that in Canada?"

Technically, the war was over with the Pretoria accords of 2002 backed by the UN and the so-called international community. Congo, it was said, would no longer be the killing fields of foreign countries and ethnic militias. This election for president and national parliament, the first in 40 years, was held peacefully and fairly on 30 July, 2006. The 19,000-member MONUC force, charged with maintaining order, brilliantly supported the complex Congo-operated voting process. The UN spent more than $500 million, the biggest peacekeeping mission in its history. But for an area of 2.5 million sq kms, the mission is tiny. White European Kosovo, by contrast, had 40,000 troops in 10,000 sq km and far fewer people. And MONUC further lacks the ability to move freely outside town centres, while warring militias still operate openly and freely in the dense forests of the East.

Already, however, some of the more influential UN member states complain about costs, what with another big mission under way in Lebanon and the horrendous needs of Darfur and western Sudan. The MONUC mandate expires this year and diplomats worry that it will be drastically reduced or cut altogether. The auspicious vote is fragile and the fear is widespread that more conflict faces this already devastated former Belgian colony.

The influential Catholic and Protestant churches called on the two presidential rivals to meet and talk. A runoff election on 29 October between the two candidates with the most number of votes – interim President Joseph Kabila and interim vice-president and former rebel leader and Mobutuist, Jean-Pierre Bemba, to achieve the necessary 50 percent majority, is a threatening omen.

As soon as the first results were announced, violence struck the capital, Kinshasa, and parts of the volatile and populous East. And will the losers accept defeat or will they return to the bush wars manipulated by foreign economic and political interests? And will the thugs in all the countries that surround Congo leave it alone?

And does western-style democracy work in a country which has never known democracy in 46 years of independence?

There is no place more pivotal to the future of Africa than Congo. Since the first of two wars broke out in 1996, its potential to drag down the prospects of the continent is immense. Of the armies of the eight African countries that were involved at the height of the war, which gave them the chance to indulge in a frenzy of looting diamonds and other rich mineral resources, several still have influence through proxy militia, mafia-style business networks and ethnic links. The DRC's instability immediately threatens Uganda,

Rwanda and Burundi – all emerging from various forms of violent unrest – and the six other countries that border Congo.

After the 2002 peace deal, a fragile, transitional government came to power, in a uniquely Congolese power-sharing arrangement imposed by the international community led by the United States and South Africa: President Kabila (thrust into the job at age 29 after the assassination of his father Laurent Kabila in 2001) shared power with four vice-presidents – the major warlords whose militias wrought havoc for the past years. (A wry Congolese joke describes this unwieldy coalition as "four plus one equals zero.")

This was peace enough to placate international donors, who've poured in money to prop up the flimsy and corrupt government and maintain some stability to reassure adventurous international mining companies, who are rushing to re-open shop in Congo.

Coltan was one of the products that grabbed the world's attention in DRC. An ore called Columbite-tantalite – coltan for short – it was one of the world's most sought-after materials although some of its sheen has now worn off. Refine coltan and you get a highly heat-resistant metal powder called tantalum, essential for cell phones and other high-tech instruments.

The link between bloodshed and resource extraction was slow to cause alarm in the West despite high-level reports from the UN. And despite international pressure, few multinational or regional corporations will grapple with the possibility that their products may contain the tainted fruits of civil strife. According to the UN, more than 20 international mineral trading companies import minerals from the Congo via Rwanda alone.

"So, don't kid yourself, my man," explodes a Kisangani businessman, Mokeni Ekopi Kane, one night in the airport at the centre of the Congo. "This war is about one thing and one thing alone. Plunder, loot, exploitation and you [Westerners] are the beneficiaries."

It's always been that way. When DRC was called Zaire – after it was called the Congo when it got independence in 1960 from Belgium who had had raped its resources and murdered 10 million people since 1890 in the world's largest ever genocide – its dictator Mobutu Sese Seko was often feted in the White House for his pro-American stance during the cold war and for his generosity in giving away contracts to American (and Canadian, European and Australian) mining corporations.

In the Ronald Reagan years, Zaire received almost half of all foreign aid allocated by the US to the entire continent. After Mobutu had pillaged the country for 30 years, a middle-aged rebel, Laurent Kabila, long a puppet of Uganda and Rwanda, finally kicked him out in 1997. Mobutu died the next year in exile, with between $5 and $8 billion stashed in foreign banks and French and Swiss properties – this while the country had fewer than 30 miles of paved roads.

The "fat cats" of Kinshasa can buy a Mercedes for a million dollars today, or a box of Kellogg's Cocoa Pops for $35 or a can of Diet Coke for $7. Per capita income, which is meaningless in DRC, is said to be $1 a day. But the Central Bank has no money.

So, who buys these items at City Market, an American style supermarket in downtown Kinshasa? The people of the Eastern Congo who loathe the politicians and businessmen of the capital 2,000 km away call them the "fat cats" whose corruption and tastes for high living have made Kinshasa the Sodom and Gomorrah of Africa. It is their SUVs along with those of embassies, relief agencies, adventurist mineral developers and the UN, that are parked outside City Market, just like at Chez Gaby, a popular Portuguese restaurant with a well-stocked bar.

Just outside the supermarket compound, the grotty streets steam and stink with garbage, and AIDS, malaria and other diseases kill many of the city's eight million or so poverty-stricken people.

According to the International Rescue Committee (IRC), 1,250 people still die every day from war-related causes, the vast majority succumbing to diseases and malnutrition that wouldn't exist but for the wars. And, beyond Kinshasa, there is little sign the war is ended.

The countryside is broken, its peoples divided and volatile. There is no rebuilding, no phone service, no electrical grid, no roads; hospitals, when they are still standing, have been looted of everything from beds to bandages. No government employee – teachers, judges, nurses, doctors, civil servants – has been properly paid in 14 years. Bribery is employed instead of taxation.

Congolese soldiers, also often unpaid or their wages appropriated by their officers, are driven to loot with robbery and violence too. There are an estimated 33,000 child soldiers, forced into militias when they are as young as 10, accomplished dead-eyed killers at 14. Amnesty International says 40 percent of these children are girls or young women kept as sex slaves. Most of the DRC, especially the East, is extremely dangerous even with the big white UN vehicles constantly on patrol. The place is on edge.

Yet Congo's troubles never hit the daily newspaper columns of the world's mass media, and it ranks lowest in the world on international donor lists. Ten months ago, in February of 2006, donors issued a humanitarian appeal of US$692 million for Congo. By the time of the runoff election, they had received about $100 million – $9.40 per person in need. As this book was being written, donors in one day pledged $900 million to rebuild Lebanon for the third time following Israel's lethal destruction. Last year's tsunami raised $550 for each person and donors didn't know how to spend it all.

Why is this nation, one of the most beautiful countries I have ever seen, the country of neglect even by Africa, let alone the rest of the world? To visit its trackless lands, its lush jungles, its smashed towns and cities, its hundreds of thousands of displaced who greet a visitor joyfully, is to see an incredibly brave and resourceful people. To worship for hours with joy and singing and intense prayer and liturgy in its huge brick and mud churches means we as churches cannot allow ourselves to be forced to make choices between Darfur and Congo. We, in obese comfort, have no excuse to be suffering donor fatigue. That is simply a globalized copout.

Congo represents the promise of Africa as much as its misery. We have money for a dubious war on terror, billions to destroy Iraq and save Afghanistan from itself. Is Africa somehow entitled to less for the country that lies at its very heart?

Can Congo be saved? Of course, but it did not get this way by itself and it cannot be saved by itself. One woman called Congo the broken heart of Africa. A man – both are pastors in the EEC (the Protestant Eglise du Christ au Congo) – asked if the white world would let millions more die because there is no one to listen to the story of the Democratic Republic of Congo.

Chapter One

The Black Messiah:
Patrice Lumumba

*The only thing we wanted for our country was the right to a
decent existence, to dignity without hypocrisy, to independence
without restrictions...The day will come when history will have
its say but it will not be written in Brussels, Paris or Washington, it will be our own.*

From Patrice Lumumba's farewell letter to his wife, Pauline, "my dear
companion".

Betrayal has marked all of Congo's independence history.
Africa's first coup d'état was engineered by the US, Belgium
and apartheid South Africa, overthrowing Patrice Lumumba
after only 10 weeks as the country's first elected prime minister. A proud and democratically-minded leader who was
widely supported by his people, Lumumba was arrested
because of unsubstantiated concerns about his alleged communist leanings. It was 14 September, 1960. He was 35. On
17 January, 1961, after being tortured, he was executed.

An appalling mass of lies and betrayals have surrounded
accounts of the murder. There have been many investigations of official sources and extensive personal testimony.
While many of the principals still deny their complicity, the
research reveals a network of complicity ranging from the
Belgian government, apartheid South Africa across the
United Nations leadership, to the CIA. Chilling official
memos which detail 'liquidation' and 'threats to national
interests' are analyzed alongside macabre tales of the
destruction of evidence, placing in stark and dignified contrast Lumumba's personal strength and his quest for Pan-
African independence.

Key to all the deceit and betrayal was the role of a once
personal friend of Lumumba, an obscure Belgian Army non-
commissioned officer, who would become leader of one of
the world's most oppressive and corrupt regimes, Joseph-
Désiré Mobutu who would take Congo through its darkest
hours.

When independence was finally and reluctantly granted
in June 1960, Belgium was shocked, like most colonizers, at
the demands for self-rule that swept the country. Although
Congo is about 80 times larger than its tiny former master,

the Belgians had managed to educate fewer than 30 university graduates. Only three Africans held management level positions in the 5,000-strong civil service and there were no Congolese army officers or doctors, agronomists, engineers or other professionals. Daily life resembled that of South Africa during apartheid. One former ambassador – not a Belgian – described it bluntly: "The Belgians were awful in Congo because they had no sense of themselves. They were the Zaire of Europe, a ratty little country divided against itself, and it proved incapable of aspiring to any heights."

Lumumba's unscheduled speech at the official independence ceremonies before assembled dignitaries in the Palais de la Nation, 20 June, 1960 in Kinshasa (then predictably called Leopoldville) before King Baudouin, which described Belgian rule as "a humiliating slavery imposed by brute force", received a standing ovation and made him a hero to millions.

Just a month earlier Lumumba had been elected prime minister in the first free and democratic elections the territory had ever had. Baudouin and the Belgian court responded with a patronizing "it is up to you to show that you are worthy of our confidence." Lumumba leaped to his feet in the crowd where he had been scribbling notes:

"We have known sarcasm and insults even on this special day. We have endured blows morning, noon and night, because we were 'niggers'... We have seen our lands despoiled under the terms of what was supposed to be the law of the land but which only recognized the rights of the strongest. We have seen that the law was quite different for a white man than for a black: accommodating for the former, cruel and inhumane for the latter. We have seen the terrible suffering of those banished to remote regions because of their political opinions or religious beliefs, exiled within their own country, their fate worse than death itself... And finally who can forget the volleys of gunfire in which so many of our brothers perished, the cells where the [Belgian] authorities threw those who would not submit to a rule where justice means exploitation and oppression."

Lumumba's speech set off alarm bells in Western capitals. The neophyte prime minister made it clear that political independence was meaningless without economic independence and the new Republic of Congo must cease being an economic colony as well. Belgian, British and American corporations had by then vast investments in the resource-rich country and they demanded the same "security" they had enjoyed in Belgian Congo. Lumumba, a tall, intense, thin man was born in 1925 in Kasai province and became a postal worker in Stanleyville (now Kisangani) and was active as a journalist and union member. He was a charismatic speaker with an almost supernatural ability to win round his audience and his message could not be contained within the boundaries of Congo.

He was inspired by the Pan-Africanism of Ghana's Kwame Nkrumah and Guinea's Ahmed Sekou Touré. His message, Western governments feared, was contagious. Flamboyant and bubbling with ideas, he was released from jail to attend the first meetings in Brussels to discuss independence, brimming with resentment over Western imperialism in Africa. Moreover, he could not be bought, although other more malleable Congolese at the Belgian round table were ready and willing to accept Western dollars and bribes.

The Brussels meetings between 20 January and 20 February, 1960, were forced on Belgium after mass demonstrations in Leopoldville in 1959 were bloodily suppressed by the Force Publique. During the Brussels negotiations both the Americans and the Soviets showed deep interest in the outcome. Contacts were made and the Americans alleged that the Russians were in touch with every member of the various Congolese delegations at the round table conference, planning to recruit the best and the brightest to use the Congo as a stepping stone into Africa. Immediately the Americans started their own recruiting drive. The cold war mentality was frigid and in Belgium's haste to shed its ungrateful colony all hell broke loose. Congo's troops mutinied when they were told there would be no move to Africanize the exclusively white officer corps. Whites were attacked and beaten and the Belgian technicians who ran the country's administration headed for the airport.

In one of a number of political miscalculations, Lumumba appointed his friend Mobutu as army chief of staff who then persuaded the troops to return to barracks. In the meantime, Lumumba faced another crisis. Belgian paratroopers landed in what the Congolese assumed was a second colonial takeover in order to assure Belgium and its western allies continued access to Congo's mineral wealth. First, copper-producing Katanga province seceded, followed by then dia-mond-rich Kasai province. The UN, under the activist Dag Hammarskjold, responded with unheard of speed, as did hordes of journalists, showing the measure of hope the West was pinning on Africa during those years. Impossible as it is to imagine in 2006, when the renewed threat of national Congolese fragmentation raises hardly a flicker of interna-tional interest, the Congo of the 1960s was one of the world's biggest news stories. Lumumba and the lackadaisi-cal President Joseph Kasavubu called in the UN, hoping it would not only protect the country from foreign aggres-sion but also help to snuff out the secession movements in the south. In another betrayal, the UN mandate refused to allow the blue berets to interfere in Congo's internal con-flicts.

Feeling betrayed, Lumumba turned to the Soviet Union for help, requesting planes, trucks and weapons to wipe out the breakaway movements, especially in rich Katanga down south near Zambia. Nikita Khrushchev obliged but his mili-tary aid came too late to prevent a bloody debacle in Kasi where the Congolese army slaughtered hundreds of Luba. But for Washington this was a dangerous ratcheting up of the cold war game. The CIA chief in Kinshasa wrote that "it was clearly an effort for the Soviets to take over and if they got control of the Congo they could have all of Central Africa. All nine of the bordering countries had their prob-lems. If the Soviets could have gotten control of the Congo, they could have used it as a base, bringing in Africans, train-ing them in sabotage and sending them home to do their duty. I determined to stop that." Lawrence Devlin was the CIA chief who had what diplomats even then described as a peculiarly close relationship to Mobutu.

Although Devlin admitted officially that Lumumba was not a communist, Washington thought he was showing a worrying resemblance to Fidel Castro. The arrival of the Soviet troops ended the strained relationship between Kasavubu and Lumumba. In a rather bizarre episode, different radio stations announced that the prime minister and the president had sacked each other and ordered the army to arrest their rival. The Russians were both brutal and stupid and some, like Mobutu, feared they would recolonize the country.

Recently released cable traffic of August 1960 shows that Devlin received authorization to "replace Lumumba with a pro-Western group" and he turned to Mobutu, Lumumba's old friend, who was easily bought by Western embassies who were helping to pay his fractious troops. The eventual outcome was that Mobutu "neutralized" both Kasavubu and Lumumba, expelled the Soviet bloc personnel and "saved" Congo for the West. The two legal leaders went into house arrest but the CIA was bent on dealing with the Lumumba problem. Several totally bizarre plans were hatched, including poisoning his toothpaste, assassinating him by snipers with high-powered rifles using freelance hit men. All proved impossible, so the CIA and Devlin supported corrupt anti-Lumumba elements within the factionalized Congo government, convinced they would do the job eventually.

But it was clear he had to go and both Belgium and the United States kept the pressure on. Lumumba, his massive energy tethered under house arrest, was becoming paranoid and afraid he would never be able to fulfill that which the Congo people had elected him to do. And so he escaped on 27 November, 1960, another unwise move since he was aware of a memorandum from Washington to King Baudouin dated 19 October, 1960, that he should be "neutralized, if possible physically". Lumumba was soon caught and transferred from his villa to a military prison. His enemies circled with steady pressure and funds were channelled from Devlin and the CIA and Belgian intelligence. South African mercenaries were also involved.

One of Lumumba's many enemies under western influence was Moise Tshombe, another was Kasavubu. They and the government commissioners turned a badly tortured and beaten Lumumba over to his enemies, specifically Tshombe, leader of breakaway Katanga. On the Belgian flight to Elizabethville (now Lubumbashi) the escorting soldiers beat their prisoners so brutally the crew locked themselves in the cockpit. On arrival, the Congo's democratically elected prime minister and two associates were taken to be killed by firing squad, watched over by Tshombe and senior Katangese government officials. The secessionists did the dirty work that the CIA and Belgium wanted done.

Mobutu always denied his role but there are stories of Lumumba asking to address the troops while he was in prison. Mobutu refused as commander. "Is it you, Joseph, saying that?" Lumumba is quoted as saying in a sad quiet voice. And Mobutu is said to have replied "Yes, it is me. I have had enough." One more betrayal. Devlin says he wasn't there and didn't know about the flight to Elizabethville. Mobutu, the corrupt pragmatist defeated his friend, the more politically sophisticated, idealistic, charismatic Lumumba. But Lumumba lacked pragmatism and that was Mobutu's forte in the early days at least.

Lumumba's body has never been found. Most stories say he was hacked to bits, his head dissolved in a vat of sulphuric acid by a Belgian team sent in to remove all traces of the assassination. Mobutu stayed in the background during five more years of political turmoil with weak and divided civilian governments. Belgium and America claimed for 40 years they had no part in the assassination, saying it was exclusively a Congolese affair. But, in 2001 Belgium finally admitted to an official inquiry "its share of responsibility", implicating the US and apartheid South Africa.

The US wanted Kasavubu as president and Tshombe as prime minister but they did not want a coup d'état. They could not agree on any strategy and in 1964 rebellion broke out in Eastern Congo, a Lumumba stronghold. Within three months more than 20,000 people were killed and Leopoldville lost control of more than half the country.

A Peoples Republic of the Congo was set up at Stanleyville (Kisangani) with support from China, Algeria, Cuba and

Egypt. Once again the US and Belgium came to the rescue of the Kasavubu-Tshombe government with help from Rhodesian and South African mercenaries and anti-Castro Cubans who beat down the Lumumbuists and the rebels, leaving behind a terrible trail of repression and plunder. Overall more than a million Congolese died in the 1964 rebellion. In 1965 as the politicians bickered in Leopoldville, Mobutu stepped in for the second time as army commander, suspended all political activity, assumed the presidency for himself and stayed for a very long time – 32 years.

The important point in the Lumumba story, briefly related, is this: he proved that the legitimacy of a post-colonial regime in Africa relates mainly to its legal mandate; but even more, that legitimacy relates to the regime's credentials as a representative of a genuine nationalism fighting against the intrigues of neo-colonialism. This is why Lumumba was, and is still, extolled by the majority as this "best son of Africa", this "Lincoln of the Congo", this "Black Messiah", whose struggle was made noble by his unswerving demand for centralism against all forms of balkanization and rendered heroic by his unyielding resistance to the forces of neo-colonialism which finally killed his body, but not his spirit.

This man, who now emerges from history as an iconic combination of statesman, sage, poet and martyr, wrote his name on the scroll of African history during his short and unhappy lifetime.

Chapter Two

Les Pillages:
Joseph-Désiré Mobutu

The All-Conquering Warrior Who, Because of His Endurance and Inflexible Will to Win, will Go from Conquest to Conquest Leaving Fire in His Wake – official translation of Lingala title given Mobutu by himself: *Mobutu Sese Seku Koko Ngbendu wa za Banga*. Literal translation: *The Cock Who Jumps on Anything That Moves*.

When Joseph-Désiré Mobutu became president of the Congo, copper, cobalt and diamonds had replaced rubber as the country's most valuable resources. In 1965, copper prices were rising and, as a result, the Congo was known world-wide as having the potential to become one of the richest countries in Africa. It still has. Yet Mobutu's unelected ascension to power initiated an era of corruption and plunder that was to see no equal on the continent.

Assuming a role akin to that of a national chief, he and his cronies devised a system of patronage that massively enriched himself and his tribe, the Ngbandi, and its local chieftains. By offering outright bribes in return for loyalty, he brought potential rivals to the feasts of his sumptuous table while those who refused to partake in the repast were murdered or imprisoned.

He cut a flamboyant figure in his new country, Zaire, and set about elevating himself to a god-like status. He dubbed himself, in addition to his official name, the Messiah, the Sun President, the Guide. He developed a new ideology called *authenticité Africaine* and rechristened the country, dumping the name Congo for the Portuguese misunderstanding of the Kikongo word for large river, *nzere*.

His picture portrait soon appeared everywhere, even in churches – a stern bespectacled face topped by a leopard-skin hat. He banned ties and tried, with some success, to have his name substituted for God in Christian hymns. It was rumoured among some people that bullets could not penetrate his skin and that he was a sorcerer with irresistible magical powers. Mobutuism, a loose collection of anti-colonialist sayings and "wisdom" strung together into dogma, became the official state ideology. In reality it was a direct steal from Belgian colonialism which had provided a tragic example of governance: that authority confers the power to steal. And the corollary to this lesson from King Leopold II was the bigger the title, the bigger the theft.

Mobutu's ego knew no bounds but he was no stupid buffoon despite his outlandish lifestyle. He followed easily the example set by his colonial predecessor, but even he could not match the Belgian's atrocities – which raises the question of how Leopold escaped remembrance alongside Hitler and Stalin as one of the great criminals of the 20th century.

Mobutu had 11 palaces, one in each province plus his home village, Gbadolite, which had an airport runway built, capable of accommodating a Concorde aircraft which was often chartered to him, his family and entourage for shopping trips to Europe. He also had a huge yacht, the *Kamanyola*, with a helicopter pad on its prow which, in his declining years was often his sole refuge, anchored in the Congo River (then the Zaire) midway between Kinshasa and Brazzaville (the Republic of Congo).

He acquired estates all over Europe, South America and North Africa. His private fortune, consisting mainly of revenues stolen from the state treasury and humanitarian aid, was estimated at around US$8 billion while per capita income among his subjects was the equivalent of US$135-a-year.

As his long rule ran on, he skilfully played the cold war game to his personal advantage. He was probably a White House official guest more often than any other African president, revelling in the attention of state dinners and Congressional speeches, ranging from John F. Kennedy through to George H. Bush. He was justified by President Ronald Reagan as a "friendly tyrant" for his reliability as an ally during the cold war era and, as late as 1989, Mobutu visited the George Herbert Bush White House as an honoured guest and personal friend. This great relationship dated back to Bush's days as director of the CIA. Mobutu claimed he had met Bush 13 times and in 1989 as they stood on the White House South Lawn, Bush said "Zaire is among America's oldest friends and its president – President Mobutu – is one of our most valued friends." Even more fulsomely: "We are proud and very pleased to have you with us today."

Within 10 years of seizing power, what infrastructure the Belgians had left behind crumbled and much of the country returned to the bush: roads decayed into impassable tracks, electricity and potable running water disappeared even in cities. Hospitals closed or had no equipment, it was all stolen while staff were unpaid. River transport was destroyed and employment was lower than at independence. Police, army and civil servants went unpaid and what wages were paid were worth only 10 percent of their 1960 values.

In the image of Leopold, Mobutu looted the copper and cobalt wealth of Shaba province for the benefit of himself and his cronies in Canadian and American industries, to the point where industrial-scale mining almost ceased. His out-sized Leopoldian appetites and ambitions grew like an addiction. His allies were not simply the mining companies, nor even the Belgians and Americans. They included the World Bank and the International Monetary Fund (IMF), various UN agencies and a clutch of humanitarian aid agencies who poured money into the country under pressure from the American government. In the 1980s, for example, the US put almost half their allotment of foreign aid to all of Africa into Zaire and hence directly into Mobutu's swelling European bank accounts.

After his coup in 1965, Mobutu offered a generous investment code, aimed at exploiting Congo's riches by foreign investors. During a 1970 visit to Richard Nixon, the president extolled Zaire's virtues as a good place for US investment and Mobutu launched a series of grandiose projects such as a steel mill near Leopoldville, a giant dam at Inga on the lower reaches of the Congo River with a long-distance power line to Katanga. More than US$2 billion was committed. Today these projects have crumbled into disuse.

Mobutu's cold warrior stance pleased the US but it was a costly alliance. Close advisors of Presidents Lyndon Johnson and Nixon told inquiries that Mobutu received at least US$150 million from the CIA alone in the first decade of his rule. Not wanting to be left out of this Central African bonanza and the power that went with it, Belgium and France joined the US in a troika of solid commitment. When rebels invaded Shaba in 1970 from Angola, the US organized a military airlift and France parachuted Legionnaires into the southern town of Kolwezi.

Hand in hand with this military help were the votes of the troika in the World Bank and IMF. A now rueful Chester Crocker, former US assistant secretary of state for Africa, recalls that "Mobutu played us like a skilled violinist: us against the French, the French against the Belgians, the CIA against the state department." If one ally proved reluctant, Mobutu could turn to its rival. When aid showed signs of drying up, he persuaded the US to buy six months' supply of cobalt to add to its strategic reserves.

In 1979 when structural adjustment programmes (SAPs) became the World Bank's latest fad, demanding conditions for loans based on good governance, Zaire for many years was one of the few African countries that could "meet" these stringent macro-economic requirements. Bretton Woods officials would later pay a heavy price for their naivete in letting Mobutu get away with the most outrageous behaviour. "You can never underestimate the inertia of a big institution," one World Bank official posted to Zaire said afterwards. "Banks are all about cash flow. They exist to lend money. The World Bank and the IMF weren't too bothered about where the aid was going or even whether it would be repaid. Just as long as it kept flowing."

When the copper bonanza ended in 1977 and prices plummeted from US$1.40 a pound to less than US$0.50, Zaire was beset by an onrush of inflation, fuel shortages, and huge debts as well as severe disruption to commerce and agriculture caused by Mobutu's seizure of foreign-owned businesses. Repayment of foreign debts amounting to US$3 billion alarmed Western bankers so much that they rescheduled the debt when it reached more than half of the government's total revenues. More money was lent, more was siphoned off, because Mobutu knew the banks had reached a point where they could not afford to let Zaire founder.

The administration disintegrated rapidly from 1970 as corruption spread from the top, permeating every level of society. Budgets were allocated for government services that did not exist. International officials estimated that 40 percent of the government's operating budget was somehow either lost or diverted to other purposes. Jobs were fictitious, army officers pocketed the pay for their troops, who in turn extorted money from civilians, air force officers turned their planes into private transport companies. Nothing could be accomplished without a bribe.

In a blistering pastoral letter issued in 1976, Roman Catholic Archbishop Eugene Kabanga of Lubumbashi wrote:

> This thirst for money transforms men into assassins. The poor workers and unemployed are condemned to misery along with their families because they are unable to pay off the person who hires. How many children and adults die without medical care because they are unable to bribe the medical personnel who are supposed to care for them? Why are there no medical supplies in the hospitals, while they are found in the marketplace? How did they get there?
>
> Why is it that in our courts justice can only be obtained by fat bribes to the judge? Why are prisoners forgotten in jail? They have no one to pay off the judge who sits on their dossier. Why do our government offices force people to come back day after day to obtain services to which they are entitled? If the clerks are not paid off, they will not be served. Why, at the opening of school, must parents go into debt to bribe the school principal? Children who are unable to pay will have no schooling.
>
> Whoever holds a morsel of authority, or means of pressure, profits from it to impose on people, especially in rural areas. All means are good to obtain money, or to humiliate the human being.

As the cold war drew to a close, Western aid, Mobutu's main source of revenue for his private coffers, began to dry up. In 1991 and again in 1993, the army, unpaid, ran amok, looting the cities, and the civilian population joined in. Once again the troika came to his rescue. French Legionnaires and Belgian paratroopers in US aircraft took over the streets while Mobutu retreated to safety in his gigantic palace at Gbadolite, or sat it out on the yacht and watched the country burn. His Israeli-trained Presidential Guard protected him. Hyperinflation rendered the currency, the *zaire*, worthless. Revolts and disturbances began afflicting the country as regularly as the seasonal rains. Essentially Zaire was without any governance worthy of the name. At least 40 percent of Zaireans suffered from extreme chronic malnutrition. In just 25 years, from being one of the most promising countries in Africa, it had become one of the poorest on earth. Yet Mobutu's personal wealth continued to increase, coming now largely from illegal and under-the-table mineral trade and exploitation with western mining companies and neighbouring countries.

Inflation in 1994 had reached 9,800 percent, copper production, once the mainstay of the economy had fallen from 450,000 tonnes in the 1970s to 30,000 in 1994, cobalt from 18,000 tonnes to 3,000, diamond production halved and gold and diamond smuggling was rampant. Gecamines, the state controlled mining company, had been plundered and looted to a standstill.

By 1995, Mobutu was forcing Zaire through its darkest days, pillaging the remnants of wealth from a depleted land and an exhausted populace. It would seem he was nearing the end of his rope. In most important ways, Zaire ceased to exist as a state. He had, in reality, been in trouble most of his time but survived and thrived personally by killing his opponents and making billionaires of his friends, propped up by the troika and some mercenaries from as far away as Serbia. But it was an empty shell by 1996 and the country smelled of decomposition. He was no longer even interested in being the Guide or the Warrior or even president. Later we would learn he was more often in Lausanne, Switzerland, being treated for prostate cancer while staying in a US$16,0000-a-night floor of the Beau-Rivage Palace Hotel.

By 1997, there was a flag, a national anthem and a sick isolated ruler but the country was a gigantic geopolitical fiction. The French and Belgians were still ready to prop him up but the Americans had no more use for him as a cold warrior and vehemently vetoed any intervention when the rebels from the east began to appear. The international bankers were gone, so was the big aid business. Zaire was an empty pit, as the *Economist* put it, "a Zaire-sized blank on a map."

Mobutu, like Leopold whom he emulated in so many ways, had taught his people that there was only one way to do things, to steal. Something had to give and in the end it would be Mobutu. By 1997 all of Eastern Zaire, including its largest cities and richest resources, were occupied by the rebels led by Uganda and Rwanda and they were heading straight for Kinshasa. Each of the provinces was basically running its own affairs, some no longer even used Zairean currency.

An American journalist, the late Carole Collins, observed: "To visit Zaire in the last years of the Mobutu era was to enter a world of cannibal capitalism, where banks and public services and any logic of economic growth and expanding productivity had ceased to operate."

Mobutu was 66, sick and weary of the business of running government. He preferred Gbadolite to Kinshasa but his enemies would allow him no rest. Weakened by surgery and chemotherapy, he dithered over the rebellions in the two Kivu provinces while recuperating in France and Switzerland. Finally, in December 1996, he returned to Zaire but his army was as sick as he was and showed no inclination to make a stand against the rampaging rebels who were sweeping the country. In March 1997 Kisangani fell and in April, Mbuji Mayi, the diamond capital and Lubumbashi, the copper capital, were in rebel hands. Mobutu hung on aboard his yacht on the edge of Kinshasa. Growing increasingly frail but refusing to leave, he finally agreed to meet with his sworn enemy Laurent Kabila after pressure from President Bill Clinton to leave with dignity.

Kabila and Mobutu finally met on a South African navy ship moored on the Atlantic coast but nothing came of it and he fled to Gbadolite, leaving his troops on the verge of collapse. Finally he fled forever, ironically on a cargo plane owned by the Angolan rebel, Jonas Savimbi whom Mobutu had long supported. Four months later, he died ignominiously in exile in Morocco, bitter and abandoned. His successor, Laurent Kabila, was sworn in as president of the newly renamed Democratic Republic of the Congo on May 17, 1997.

Mobutu had single-handedly run the Congo since 1965; he had ridiculed his critics and his opponents with Louis XV-style warnings that after him would come the deluge. Few could really comprehend a future without the Guide at the helm. Most politicians were totally co-opted and had made a magnificent living as professional opponents. Now they trembled at the prospect of Mobutu's disappearance.

It may be an oversimplification to blame all of Africa's troubles on European imperialism. It is more complicated than that. But looking at Mobutu's 32 years and more in power, he resembled no one, except for the colour of his skin, more than the vicious monarch who owned the same territory a century earlier. Mobutu and Leopold, both killers and looters, two of the greatest villains in African history. *Les Pillages*.

Chapter Three

A Maoist with Commercial Instincts: Laurent-Désiré Kabila

Kabila's very first act after declaring himself president on 17 May, 1997 – no democratic niceties like elections here – was to restore the name Congo to the country – Zaire became the Democratic Republic of the Congo (DRC). Washington wasted no time in recognizing that reality although it had been Zaire's main supporter for 32 years. "Zaire went away on Friday afternoon with Mobutu. That country has vanished," announced the US State Department. Mobutu changed the name from Congo to Zaire in 1971 to try to erase Lumumba's enduring legacy. Some Congolese observers noted almost immediately how assiduously Kabila was following Mobutu's playbook and feared for the country's future, despite its third new name since independence and another new flag. But Washington, always the big player in DRC, was reading from Kabila's songsheet and never was a word of criticism heard from the American Embassy.

With the change in regimes, the crowd around Kinshasa's Intercontinental Hotel, built by Mobutu in 1971 as the place for the elites to be seen, changed. Kabila's ethnic allies from Katanga province formed the inner circle, or so it seemed. Others were more concerned with the discreet and much more modest Rwandans who, it was being said, already pulled the real strings. Among this disparate and colourful crowd were boy soldiers complete with AK-47s rushing up and down the hotel's elevators elbowing out of the way the carpetbagging foreign businessmen, ready to cut quick and sleazy deals for minerals with a government in need of ready cash.

Long-time, street-smart Kinois – residents of Kinshasa – began to mutter darkly that the same old Mobutu smell of corruption and dirty deals was wafting through the crowded streets. It was also noted outside that while Kabila and his sponsors entered the city, they had been careful to keep the tough Rwandan forces, who constituted the strength of the rebel army, out of the picture. But when it came to taking charge of the city and country, there was no hiding the identity of the people who held the guns and used them to tidy up the streetwalkers and remove their miniskirts which created a flap among the hedonistic Kinois. A small flap one might say, but it immediately labelled the Rwandans and their hand-picked president, with his long years in the bush, as way out of touch, out of sync with his people. They soon called him a "dombolo", a man held prisoner by his captors.

Tough-looking Tutsi agents took over security at Ndjili airport. Kabila's son, a shy boyish man of 26 with little French, who spoke mostly the Swahili of the Eastern provinces and Tanzania where he went to school, was named to lead the army. And the president himself, a portly, bald-headed, hard-drinking figure, was always surrounded by a wiry phalanx of Tutsi bodyguards. But he was smart enough to try and trace his political lineage back to Lumumba.

The administration, such as it was in those early days of transition from minor bush rebel-bandits, concentrated on dividing up the spoils from the past regime, parcelling out the spacious villas built by the Belgians on the hills of afflu-ent Binza, while schools and clinics remained closed. Congo, despite its dreadful corruption and misgovernance, was still a large, proud and potentially wealthy country of some 50 million which somehow found itself reduced to a vassal state of overcrowded and genocide-devastated Rwanda.

Congo had been ruled by dictators for much of its history, apart from the brief and sad interlude in 1960. Kabila, whose main claim to fame was that he was a professional rebel, had spent much of his time holed up in Tanzania under the discreet protection of the beloved Mwalimu Julius Nyerere with other rebels who mostly hung around Dar es Salaam bars spouting various themes of Marxism and Maoism.

In 1965, Kabila had a fleeting moment of fame when Ernesto 'Che' Guevara, the Cuban revolutionary, chose Kabila's group, which operated as a liberation movement along the western shores of Lake Tanganyika, to instill Marxism in Africa. Kabila, then 26, who had studied in Paris and Belgrade, hoped to establish a provisional govern-ment for the liberated areas of the east. Both Guevara's plan to train liberation movements and Kabila's rebel movement turned out to be a fiasco. The People's Liberation Army, as

18

it was called, was untrained, undisciplined, disorganized, riven by ethnic rivalry and petty squabbles. It spent much of its time across the lake in Kigoma, Tanzania, at the bars and brothels, rather than fighting Mobutu who had then never really heard of this force.

Guevara actually only met Kabila once, for about five days, and records in his diaries that "he was addicted to drink and women and concerned only with political squabbles." After seven months the Cuban left Africa saying the rebels were "a parasite army" that did not work, train or fight and stole its provisions and labour from the local population.

It would be many years before Kabila was heard of again except as a minor brigand who illegally trafficked in gold, diamonds and ivory and dabbled in Maoist ideology. He had changed his group's name to the Alliance of Democratic Forces for the Liberation of Congo-Zaire (AFDL).

In the meantime, President Paul Kagame, the tough-minded and ascetic Tutsi who took over Rwanda following its blood-curdling genocide of most Tutsis and some moderate Hutus, that saw at least 800,000 killed in 10 weeks of slaughter in 1994, was determined that "never again" would mean just that. Not for him the liberal maunderings of Bill Clinton who turned his back on Rwanda until the massacres were over and then tearfully apologized.

Kagame knew he had more than a million Hutus, including the worst of the Rwandan army, the *interahamwe* killers and the genocidal interim government that organized the mass ethnic killings, just across the border in refugee camps in Zaire. He also knew that Mobutu was a pal of Juvenal Habyirimana, the Hutu extremist president of Rwanda who had been shot out of the sky to signal the start of the genocide.

Kagame had to deal with this major threat on his borders. The exiles seethed with hatred, they were well-armed and wanted nothing better than to cross back into Rwanda and "finish the job" they had begun in 1994. They were living off the UN and aid agencies in huge camps on the unyielding lava beds of North Kivu province. With the connivance of Mobutu they were preparing for another blood feud with their Tutsi rivals. They rebuilt their units and prepared for the second genocide.

Kagame, with one of the best intelligence gathering groups in Africa, always knew exactly what was going on and he also knew that two years after the Rwanda genocide, the world had already begun to forget the million or more Hutus in Zaire and had no stomach to seal the porous borders with Zaire, disarm the extremists and send them home to face justice. This was no Bosnia or Kosovo, but Central Africa where life was cheap. "African solutions for African problems."

Suddenly in 1996, the politicos in Kinshasa had a crisis on their hands again and it seemed to come from nowhere. There were rumours that the Banyumulenge, a marginal ethnic group, said to be Tutsi, had started a rebellion in the east. Before anyone could figure out who they were, more than a couple of thousand kilometres from the capital, city after city was falling until even the provincial capital, Goma, was captured by rebels in shiny rubber boots with new Kalashnikovs.

In a matter of days the UN evacuated its workers from the sprawling camps, which were then emptied into the forests. Hundreds of thousands of Rwandan Hutus were on the move, fleeing from these Banyamulenge "rebels". In fact, anyone who wanted to know their history understood they were migrants from Rwanda and Burundi for many generations, including some recently. The lights went on in several capitals, not least of all Kinshasa. This was not a tribal dispute, this was a Rwandan-led campaign to empty the refugee camps and prevent a repeat of the genocide, and replace Mobutu with someone more amenable to Kagame's concerns.

And the man they chose to lead the rebellion was none other than Che Guevara's old comrade, the rotund Laurent Désiré Kabila and his AFDL. Kabila came out of his shadowy existence in Dar es Salaam proclaiming the start of a new Zairean revolution and the removal of the dictator who had dominated Central Africa for three decades. It sounded a bit ludicrous, especially coming from Kabila, and few took it seriously, least of all Mobutu and his cabal.

Although they were shocked to lose the Great Lakes to Kabila, they were beginning to realize, as was the misinformed western media, that the rebels were backed, or even led, by Rwanda and Burundi and just maybe, Uganda. It was a huge war and Mobutu was sick or dying of cancer in Europe.

Kabila, despite his unsavoury reputation as a revolutionary, was greeted with ecstasy by the long-neglected Swahili-speaking population of Eastern Zaire. The ideology was not very important. Some thought they were fighting for the overthrow of capitalism, others for the survival of the Banyamulenge, some for the end of Mobutu. The hated Zairean army cut and ran – but not before they looted, raped and murdered the local populace, even stealing all the aid agencies' material and equipment – when they came face to face with the AFDL and its Ugandan, Rwandan and Burundian allies. In their trademark rubber boots, the AFDL could hardly keep up with the Zairean army's accelerating rout.

Despite ineffectual calls by the UN and a few Western states for a ceasefire, it was soon clear there was not much of a war going on. Conquests followed a familiar pattern. The AFDL would appear on the horizon, the local officials would try hard to get the Zairean soldiers out, to avoid reprisals and further looting, and another town would fall.

Nobody got it right. In January 1997, Angola joined the anti-Mobutu onslaught (he had long supported Savimbi and now was to get his payback). Zaire's security system was rotten and fell apart as village after village welcomed the liberators. The campaign Rwanda, then Burundi and Uganda, had started – to eliminate an eastern border problem and resolve the problem of fanatical Hutu refugees – had transformed itself into something else entirely: the takeover of a vast country.

The West liked to call it a popular uprising but in reality, it was a Tutsi-driven invasion from Rwanda, with lots of support from similar ethnic groups in Uganda and Burundi. It was Kagame's game all the way. It was "never again".

Often the analogy with Israel was made – two tiny victims of holocaust – making sure they could be secure for a long time.

Nothing could stop the AFDL. Kabila refused a proposal to allow Mobutu a gradual exit with dignity because the rebels knew of the president's famous use of procrastination. The Americans came with an important delegation to talk about "Mobutu's last chance". All his old friends were there, the CIA, state department, national security council, a presidential envoy from Clinton, and they told Mobutu that Kabila had taken the last major town en route to Kinshasa and he had better step down "with honour and dignity" now. And they wanted a swift answer because they were meeting Kabila the next day.

Mobutu, tears streaming down his haggard face, told the Americans they could save him once again, and "send in your troops and stop this". They refused, guaranteeing only his personal safety. It was all over.

Kinshasa, ever pragmatic and untrustworthy, almost overnight removed the word Zaire from public buildings and road signs, leopard statues were torn down, the flaming torch of the Mobutu era was painted over with the blue and yellow of the AFDL. The rebel leader, who had promised he would retire once Mobutu was gone, moved his presidential office temporarily into the Intercontinental.

In theory, the AFDL was now in charge of one of Africa's richest states. In practice, it had inherited a country shattered almost back to the Iron Age of the 15th century when the Portuguese first arrived. Nothing worked. Its debts were US$14 billion. And, worst of all, between Leopold and Mobutu there was a population cynically led to believe that breaking the law with impunity was the only way to live.

Kabila proved that cynicism to be accurate. Some of Congo's darkest days ever began in 1997. He had won the First Congo War but would quickly lose the Second.

He was praised at his inauguration as representing a "new breed" of reform-minded African leaders. People were so relieved to see the last of Mobutu's pillaging that Kabila was called the Saviour of Central Africa. President Yoweri

Museveni of Uganda, an early ally, said he had liberated not only Congo but all of Africa. Nelson Mandela paid fulsome tributes. Kabila portrayed himself as a true successor of Patrice Lumumba, a Pan-Africanist dedicated to freedom for Congo.

But there were those who remembered the Dar es Salaam days and wondered at the transformation, especially as the wild drinking and womanizing continued apace. Quietly, people, politicians, the educated, the churches and others wondered if they had inherited another tyrant, a dictator propelled to power by accident with no political programme, no strategic vision, no experience in governance. Kabila was known for decades as secretive and paranoid. He quickly banned political opposition and surrounded himself with friends, family and above all the Rwandans. Like Mobutu, he used the intelligence apparatus to keep political control. Veteran Mobutu opponent, Etienne Tshisekedi from Kasai found himself once again arrested and sent into internal exile. Journalists were detained and Kabila started a person-ality cult like Mobutu, using one of the former dictator's chief propagandists for the task. Promised elections were never held.

The independence of the Central Bank was rescinded and given to a committee stuffed with sympathetic ministers; people began to say there was no difference between the Mobutu dictatorship and the new one. Kabila quickly alien-ated himself from aid donors and investors when he refused to begin paying down the huge debt as promised. When he blocked a United Nations investigation into the massacre of tens of thousands of Rwandan refugees during his march to power, the international community lost much faith in him too.

His control of the army had grown increasingly fragile. Soon disenchantment began to grow in Kigali, when Kagame found Congo was still being used as a base for attacks on Rwanda. In Kampala, Museveni had similar com-plaints when the notorious Lord's Resistance Army (LRA) used a DRC national park near the northern Uganda border to sow terror and mayhem among the northern Ugandan peoples. As Kabila started to assert his independence, Kagame and Museveni began plans for another regime change.

A new rebellion sprang up and was launched from the Kivu provinces of the East. *Rassemblement Congolais pour la Democratie* (RCD) was the first of the rebel groups that terrorized the eastern part of the country. Headed by another Dar es Salaam-based history teacher, Ernest Wanda dia Wamba, it included defectors from Kabila's army and a mixed bag of Mobutu politicians, Congolese Tutsis, Banyamulenge and former AFDL leaders who had been squeezed out of Kabila's inner circle. But, as in the first rebellion, the driving force was the highly skilled Rwandan army. By 1998 they had reached the edge of the capital and controlled more than half the country. The Second Congo War (1998-2003) was extremely violent and those who suffered the most were the civilian population.

Only the massive intervention of the tough Angolan army, followed by Namibian and Zimbabwean troops, saved the day for Kabila. Angola wanted to be a kingmaker and decide who would rule Kinshasa which had historically provided rear bases for UNITA guerrillas. Zimbabwe had no strategic interests or even borders with Congo but President Robert Mugabe wanted to become a regional power-broker and pick up some lucrative mining concessions for Zimbabwe and especially its powerful generals. Namibia, Sudan and Chad decided to link up with Angola while Rwanda, Uganda and Burundi stuck together to secure their borders from Hutu and other rebel groups. These interventions resulted in Africa's "World War" or "the Great War of Africa", directly involving nine African nations and at least 20 armed groups, and has killed more people than any war in the world since 1945, some 4.1 million civilians, mostly through starvation and disease. Millions more were displaced from their homes or sought asylum in neighbouring countries. Through it all, the world and most of Africa remained unaware and indifferent.

Perhaps one of the most serious long-term problems of these two conflicts is the divisions created in the once fairly cohesive country. Congo was split in half with Kabila and his foreign allies, Angola and Zimbabwe controlling Kinshasa, and Rwanda and Uganda controlling the north and east. Zimbabwean troops were hastily dispatched to Mbuji-Maya, the diamond capital, where it was paid in gems for the cost of propping up Kabila.

Like vultures picking over a dead carcass, all sides engaged in a scramble for the spoils of war. The Great African War enriched immeasurably, as much even as Mobutu had his cronies, elite groups of Angolan, Zimbabwean and Namibian army officers, corrupt politicians and crooked businessmen. Kabila handed out contracts and concessions giving Angola control of Congo's petroleum distribution and a large slice of the blood-diamond trade for its generals. Zimbabwe was brought into joint venture projects in diamonds, gold and timber and awarded a stake in Gecamines Eastern Congo, plundering it for gold, diamonds, timber, coltan, coffee, cattle and other valuable resources. The volume of loot grew in leaps and bounds, becoming the principal reason – ahead of the *interahamwe* – for them to continue their occupation. Each established separate zones of control and set up militias as partners in the enterprise. These militias ravaged the civilian population, pillaging, raping and murdering at will. The UN estimated that 70 percent of the highly lucrative coltan production in Eastern Congo was mined under the direct surveillance of the Rwandan army and shipped from airstrips near the mine sites directly to Kigali.

Kabila survived temporarily but it begs the question as to whether Congo did. It had never been a colony in the British, Portuguese and French sense. It was Leopold's estate. It had never been given a chance to be a country at independence and under Mobutu and later Kabila, it remained a personal domain. Two invasions by Rwanda and Uganda on one side and the Kabila allies on the other left the looted country a chaotic mess. The figures of death and mayhem are astounding. The Congo wars, UN estimates say, killed four million, of whom 800,000 were children five years old or younger; 400,000 women were raped, hundreds of thousands and more subsisted on berries and grubs. The country was cut off from the rest of the world without so much as an aspirin to treat the HIV/AIDs epidemic and the multitude of tropical diseases.

Africa's first great war got some international and continental attention the first time round. Kabila, succeeding the garish figure of Mobutu, had some novelty at first and was actually allowed to join the Southern African Development Community (SADC) although Congo's geo-political alliances are in central Africa. But the Western world, which makes such an abstraction of Africa, found the new show soon became a bore. Washington, especially, having experimented with its so-called "African solutions to African problems", silently recognized its failures and stayed away altogether. Slowly the forest took over, green and unimaginably thick across the waistline of the continent. Defied only by the might of the deceptively lazy river, it serves to muffle the cries of its people, once again the victims of crazed dictators.

Rwanda organized its exploitation of Eastern Congo through the army ("the Congo Desk"), gaining a grip on coltan which by 2000 was earning the tiny country US$250 million when world prices soared. The UN panel commented:

> Here lies the vicious cycle of war. Coltan has permitted the Rwandan army to sustain its presence in the Democratic Republic of the Congo. The army has provided protection and security to those individuals and companies extracting coltan [the tantalum ore used by high technology industries in the West, notably mobile telephone manufacturers]. These have made money which is shared with the army, which in turn continues to provide the enabling environment to continue the exploitation.

Uganda's system was less direct but by no means less effective. Museveni's government allowed high-ranking military officers a free rein in making fortunes, including members of the president's family. The Ugandan army enforced this business empire, aircraft arrived from nearby Ugandan airfields loaded with consumer goods and left with diamonds, gold and coltan. Congo gold became a major Ugandan export.

Both Rwanda and Uganda established militias of Congolese to act on their behalf, collect taxes and other revenues they expropriated. They brutalized the people of towns like Bunia, Beni and Butembo and their surrounding villages. Eastern Congo – North and South Kivu provinces and Ituri – has been described by Human Rights Watch as the "bloodiest corner in Africa". In the early part of the 21st century, the entire eastern region became a battleground as militias set up by Uganda and Rwanda splintered into factions of competing armies, looting, raping and killing at will. The genocide in Rwanda and the civil wars in Burundi were fought over again in Congo, especially in Kivu. *Interahamwe* and former Rwandan army militias were helped by Zimbabwe. The regular Rwanda army retaliated with coercion and massacres. Hutu rebel groups were also trained by Zimbabwe in Katanga to attack Burundi from bases in Kivu. Burundi rebels fought as mercenaries in Kabila's army, along with contingents of *interahamwe* to help defend strategic towns like Lubumbashi and Mbuji-Maya.

In former Orientale province, and especially Ituri, rival militias armed by Uganda clashed repeatedly over control of gold, diamonds and coltan sites. A savage tribal war broke out between Hema pastoralists and Lendu farmers with long-standing grievances over cattle and land. Both groups were armed by Uganda for its own reasons. Another Uganda-backed group, *Mouvement pour la Libération du Congo* (MLC) was led by Jean-Pierre Bemba, a millionaire businessman with close ties to Mobutu. It opened up a front, gaining control of the north, and later Bemba, although charged with war crimes, would become the closest rival for the 2006 presidential election against Joseph Kabila.

The violent scramble for Congo's wealth reached a climax in 2000 when Rwanda and Uganda fought three huge battles for control of Kisangani and its lucrative diamond trade. These wars, so far from their borders with Congo, ended the pretence that their presence in Eastern Congo was to protect their borders from homegrown rebels. Rwanda, the victim of a genocide, began to look like a predator and Museveni, hailed by the US as an example of a "new breed" of disciplined African leader, led a country just like the old-fashioned predators. The UN belatedly demanded that both countries leave the DRC and ordered an investigation into the illegal exploitation of Congo's wealth. By this time Kabila controlled about a third of his country, Rwanda and Uganda most of the north and east.

Outside of Africa, most states remained neutral, but urged an end to the violence. Non-African states were extremely reluctant to send troops to the region. A number of Western mining and diamond companies, most notably from the US, Canada and Israel, supported the Kabila government in exchange for business deals. These actions attracted substantial criticism from human rights groups.

Negotiations began but largely failed, mainly because of Kabila's obstruction and his increasingly close ties to the authoritarian Robert Mugabe who was the most ardent supporter of intervention, lured by Congo's rich natural resources and a desire to increase his own power and prestige in Africa. Kabila and Mugabe had signed a US$200 million contract involving corporations owned by Mugabe and his family, and there were several reports in 1998 of numerous mining contracts being negotiated with companies under the state mining company. A UN study charged that over a three-year period more than US$5 billion of Congo's assets were transferred from the state mining sector to private companies without payment of any kind.

For their part, Rwanda and Uganda, having failed to dislodge Kabila from his Kinshasa enclave turned resource-rich Eastern Congo into their own private business area.

Nevertheless, some faltering diplomatic talks contributed to the first cease-fire of the war. In July 1999, the Lusaka Ceasefire Agreement was signed by the six warring countries (DRC, Angola, Namibia, Zimbabwe, Rwanda and Uganda) but several militias refused to sign. Under the agreement, forces from all sides, under a Joint Military Commission, would cooperate in tracking, disarming and documenting all armed groups in the Congo, especially those forces identified with the 1994 Rwandan genocide. Few provisions were made to actually disarm the militias.

In early 2000, the UN authorized a force of 5,537 troops, known by the French acronym MONUC, to monitor the cease-fire. However, fighting continued between rebels and government forces, and between Rwandan and Ugandan forces. Numerous clashes and offensives occurred throughout the country.

On 16 January 2001, Laurent Kabila was shot at close range and killed by one of his young bodyguards. It is unknown who ordered the killing but most feel Kabila's allies were to blame as they were tired of his duplicity, in particular his failure to implement a detailed timetable for the introduction of a new democratic constitution leading to free and fair elections. The assassin was caught and executed on the spot by a cousin of Kabila and was never interrogated. In a bizarre twist, the mortally wounded president was flown to Harare by Zimbabwe aircraft although he died en route. It was 36 hours before the Congolese would know of his death.

Unable to agree on a successor, his cronies allowed the Congolese parliament to pick his 30-year-old son, Joseph, to be sworn in as president to replace his father. The powerful and rarely subtle hand of Mugabe was widely noted, along with the fact that most parliamentarians had been hand-picked by the elder Kabila. In February, the new president met Kagame in the US and soon afterwards the rebels agreed to a UN pullout plan. Shortly thereafter Uganda and Rwanda began pulling troops back.

Once again Congo was back where it had been, another president murdered, an unelected parliament and undemocratically chosen fourth president, and more than three million civilians and some soldiers had died, mostly from disease, starvation and war damage, the largest death toll in African history. And the carnage was far from over. In Eastern Congo the rival militias, usually surrogates for Uganda and Rwanda under the control of warlords, gave little respite from the violence, rape, murder and pillage. Although a ceasefire was supposed to be in place, another million civilians would die in a situation of utter desperation, ignored by the world and by their own neighbours, stripped of their wealth, their human rights, their very existence.

A number of attempts to end the violence were made, but it was not until 19 April, 2002, that an agreement was signed at Sun City in South Africa which called for a unified, multi-party government and democratic elections. Critics noted that there were no stipulations regarding the unification of the army, which weakened the effectiveness of the agreement. The same year Rwanda and DRC signed a peace deal calling for the withdrawal of 20,000 Rwandan soldiers, the arrest of former Rwandan soldiers and dismantling of the *interahamwe*.

Still later in 2002 the Luanda Agreement formalized peace between Congo and Uganda. The treaty aimed to get Uganda to withdraw its troops from the northeast, especially Ituri province, but implementation proved troublesome.

An agreement to set up a transitional government was signed on 17 December, 2002, by the domestic political opposition, various militias and political parties, and representatives of civil society (mainly the churches) that, it was hoped, would result in legislative and presidential elections within two years and would mark the formal end of the Second Congo War.

The Agreement established a transitional government headed by an interim president and four vice-presidents representing the main warring factions. The government was obliged by the agreement to reunify the country, disarm and integrate the warlords and hold elections. There were numerous problems, resulting in continued instability in much of the country and a delay in the scheduled national elections from June 2005 to July 2006.

The main cause of the continued weakness of the transitional government is the refusal by the former warring parties to give up power to a centralized and neutral national administration. All belligerents maintain administrative and military structures separate from that of the transitional government. A high level of official corruption, siphoning money away from civil servants, soldiers and infrastructure projects causes further instability.

The fragility of the state has allowed continued violence and human rights abuses in the east. There are four significant centres of conflict: North and South Kivu, Ituri and Katanga.

Joseph Kabila was born in the mountains of Fizi in Eastern Congo in 1971, the eldest son of the sometime rebel leader Laurent-Désiré and Mahanya Sifa, a Tutsi. He grew up in Dar es Salaam, speaking English and Swahili instead of French and Lingala, DRC's lingua franca. His political enemies say he cannot become president because he is not Congolese, other detractors say he is not Laurent's legitimate son.

He seldom makes speeches, rarely gives press conferences and seldom even campaigned in public during the 2006 run-up to voting, He is said to be shy and reserved, in contrast to the usually talkative and effusive Congolese. But his handlers claim that it is his Swahili cultural background to be polite. He finished secondary school in Tanzania and then took military training in Rwanda, Uganda and later, China. Then he joined his father's AFDL as operations commander in the First Congo War.

When he decided to run for the presidency in the 2006 elections, Kabila was constitutionally too young and so an amendment was passed during the 2005 constitutional referendum lowering the age for a president from 35 to 30. Originally, he registered as an independent for the election but is now known as one of the founders of the People's Party for Reconstruction and Democracy (PPRD) which chose him as their presidential candidate.

On his 2006 presidential campaign posters, a gleaming, handsome Joseph Kabila, clad in a well-cut business-like dark blue suit, looking every inch the potential head of state says, in the many languages of the Democratic Republic of Congo: "The Congolese people know exactly where their interests are. There is a reason to hope."

The tens of millions of sufffering and sick Congolese people are hoping he is right and that he will keep reminding the "boys", as the new politicians are known, that they are in politics to serve and change the lives of the 60 million or more people of this battered and abused nation.

Chapter Four

Beyond the Bullets and the Blades: The Women and Children

Their names were Innocent. Two boys in a small Anglican hospital, not far from the border between Congo and Rwanda. One was 14, the other 12. They were not related, but both represent the violence of war and the many ways in which the silent onslaught in Eastern Congo destroys society and kills the most vulnerable, children and women.

The older of the two Innocents was the most obvious victim of the violence of war. He had been chopped with a machete all around his head and neck as he tried to run away from *interahamwe* militias who raided his village early in 2006. His mother was killed. He arrived at the hospital in his father's arms. He was rushed into the small ill-equipped surgery and his wounds sutured and bandaged. Doctors were not sure he would live. He was unconscious when I saw him.

The other Innocent was also from a nearby village overrun by militias, a different gang but also backed by the Ugandan army. He got away and avoided injury. He ran with his family and other villagers and eventually got to a camp, an IDP camp. IDP is the acronym given to people the UN and aid agencies call Internally Displaced Persons. They become statistics, IDPs, not persons. These camps are scattered all over Eastern Congo, wet, dirty, disease-ridden places where frightened people live on emergency rations that are always too short. Some have little schools, others have a makeshift clinic. Most have neither. Many huddle, rib-thin and ill in ragged second-hand clothing – the largesse of the West's castoffs – under the blue plastic sheeting given out by UNHCR.

This 12-year old Innocent settled into an IDP camp that was supposed to be temporary, but he was there for two years before aid workers got him to the hospital. His skinny body was still covered in mosquito bites when I visited him and his blood full of the parasites that cause malaria, a disease that can be cured but that kills around a million Africans every year if untreated, which is almost always the case in war zones like Ituri province. His survival was still uncertain but he will likely live because he got to the hospital. But doctors told me that he will almost surely get malaria again and again and who knows if there will be a hospital when next he needs one.

There are other diseases too that kill villagers in the terrible wars around the Congo. Diseases like measles, meningitis or AIDS. The UN's humanitarian chief, Jan Egeland, has called rape and sexual abuse in the DRC "a cancer that seems to be out of control and spreads the virus (HIV) that causes the lethal disease, AIDS."

The 2006 annual AIDS conference held in Toronto was told how rape is used as a weapon of war in DRC. About 2,000 Ugandan and Rwandan soldiers, already infected with the deadly virus, were conscripted to rape women and children in the DRC in 1998-99 in an appalling attempt to deliberately spread HIV. According to a report presented to the 16th annual conference and written by professors from Canada's McMaster University and the world-famous Johns Hopkins University in the US, a complaint has been filed by Congo's interim government with the African Commission on Human and Peoples Rights against Uganda and Rwanda for planning to start an AIDS pandemic to decimate the local population. Professors Ed Mills and Jean Nachega wrote: "About 2,000 AIDS-suffering or HIV-positive Ugandan soldiers were sent to the front in the eastern province of Orientale with the mission of raping girls and women so as to propagate an AIDS pandemic among the local population." Should that not be called genocide or at least a crime against humanity?

Both the governments of Rwanda and Uganda have denied the allegations. Professor Nachega of Johns Hopkins said some children as young as one and two-years-old had been raped by the infected militias.

Egeland told the UN Security Council on 15 September, 2006 that he was shocked by the stories of women who had been raped by members of the Congolese army and militia groups. He said the best estimates available were that somewhere around 40,000 women were raped each month, especially in the two Kivu provinces and Ituri. Mutilations often followed the rapes.

These harrowing experiences were told to me by women I met in Goma in North Kivu Province and Bukavu in South Kivu. It is the story of village women, rape and sexual violence, a heroic doctor and the incredible will to live and recover from endless gang rape, insertion of guns and tree branches into the women's vaginas and the loss of husbands, children, friends and relatives as rape victims are banished with more violence from their village homes. "Go live with your rapist," Therese's husband said and threw her out of their hut and village.

Panzi General Hospital's gynaecological wards in Bukavu reek from women with fistula: rips in the vaginal wall where rapists tore out chunks of flesh separating the bladder and rectum from the vagina. Women with fistula have no control over their bodily functions.

She was gang-raped by Rwanda-backed militia who plundered her village. Lillianne is about 40. It took her a year to walk 60 kms to Panzi, blood-soaked rags clamped between her thighs as she walked, her wounds oozing blood, infection and waste. She had bananas and groundnuts to trade and eat as she struggled along, alone. She had walked 40 km and had just enough money to pay for lifts in trucks for the last 20.

Finally, she arrived at Panzi Hospital in 2003, thin, sick, and took her place in line, along with 80 other women, waiting for surgery – sometimes four and five operations – by Dr Denis Mukwege, the only doctor who knows how to treat this fistula and only one of two doctors at Panzi, a hospital run by *L'Eglise du Christ au Congo* (ECC) and supported by overseas partners like ACT International, the ecumenical emergencies organization.

Mukwege and one other doctor are the only gynaecological surgeons in the whole Eastern Congo who can perform such reconstructive surgery and he can repair only five women a week. The air is thick with flies and smells terribly... Yet Lillianne is happier than she's been in years.

"Until I came here, I had no hope I could be helped," she says. Her husband threw her out, her friends said she stank. Her family rejected her. She was alone in the thick forest.

The International Rescue Committee estimates there are probably 40,000 women like her in DRC.

Across the DRC are tens of thousands of women like this: physically ravaged, emotionally terrorized, financially impoverished. Except for Lillianne and a few fortunate others, these women have no help of any kind: years of war have left the country in ruins, and Congolese women have been victims of rape on a scale never seen before. Every one of dozens of armed groups in this war has used rape as a weapon. Amnesty International (AI) researchers believe there has been more rape here than in any other conflict, but the actual scale is still unknown.

"They rape a woman, five or six, or more of them at a time – but that is not enough. Then they shoot a gun into her vagina," says Dr Mukwege. "In all my years here, I never saw anything like it. … [T]o see so many raped, that shocks me, but what shocks me more is the way they are raped."

Each armed group has a trademark manner of violating, he explains. The Burundians rape men as well as women. The Mai Mai – local defence forces – rape with branches or bayonets, and mutilate their victims. The Rwandans, like those who attacked Lilliane, set groups of soldiers to rape one woman.

Dr Mukwege, a tall, well-built surgeon, is a committed Pentecostal Christian. He describes how it began for him in 1999 "with a growing plague of sexual violence; I think I saw 48 women in 1999, then the next year 2,120; today 3,600 women are finding their way to Panzi through the bush, at least 10 every day of the week. It is utterly horrible." Across Lake Kivu at Goma, another hospital, Heal Africa, or "Docs" for short, treats a similar number of patients with fistula and has 132 women whose needs are not just the physical agony of insanely violent rape but are heavily traumatized, malnourished, victims of war beyond belief. Some are not even teenagers, some have been at Docs since 1996; they have nowhere to go.

Of the 10 who arrive every day, at least 30 percent need immediate, complex and difficult surgery. The other 70 percent need long hours of physical and emotional treatment.

Almost all require psychological support. Many never stop screaming, others squat facing a wall staring endlessly into space. Some giggle madly.

"This is not just classic violence against women," says Dr Mukwege, this rape in Eastern Congo is a well-planned strategy of war by the invading armies and the militias they support from Uganda, Rwanda and Burundi, it is planned by the Congolese army and police, it is part of the destruction of our people." He shakes his head, almost in bewilderment, and continues: "Women are raped in front of their husbands and children in public places. Everyone is terrified and traumatized. Husbands then leave their wives, children are left alone, families are torn apart, the violence breaks down the society. It is a huge scandal, the use of rape and sexual violence and HIV/AIDS. It is cruelty in a spectacular way, shooting into the vagina, using knives to cut women's sexual organs."

Since 1999, Dr Mukwege has treated 19,000 women and these are only the most serious cases. "I cannot imagine how many don't get to us but it is many… many never get to health centres. When peace comes, if it ever comes, we will see many more. More than 50 percent of the women will never have children again. I have a hundred cases of women who are so brutally smashed that surgery will never make them continent again."

A profoundly spiritual man and a skilled surgeon, Dr Mukwege worries deeply about the long-term impacts of the trauma on the whole society, especially rural society. "These women come and they are made to feel guilty for being raped because they are the property of their husbands. Sometimes they commit suicide, sometimes the husbands commit suicide, they are so humiliated. There is no one to take care of the women, they are soon mentally ill. Think of the ones 8-10-12-years-old who cannot control their faeces, their urine – they are finished for life, they smell so they aren't allowed home, they lose their childhood and adolescence. We have only 120 beds for 500 patients, they can't stay here. We need long-term places but there is no money."

When Dr Mukwege has finished, we cannot speak anymore. How long can he go on? I finally ask.

"As long as God wills it. I can't understand it, I can't comprehend it, these are our neighbour countries. I am haunted by the children who are raped and diseased, how will they go on?

"When I have my first consultation with these battered girls and women, I am shocked after all these years. I am so shocked now that I don't want to hear the stories, each one gets worse. It makes me so sad and I get sick. I can only try not to think of how sick mankind is. It is awful."

We embrace, this big, strong-looking surgeon who believes his faith so deeply, and the journalist who has seen too much pain for too many years. Our eyes lock, we turn away, he to his surgery and I to talk to the women in one of the wards, their cots covered in mosquito nets, their cheery smiles when a newcomer arrives. "Jambo san," they call out cheerfully in Swahili, "muzuri," I say. But it is through tears.

There is fear in the voices of the women we meet almost everywhere. There is also rage and there is total confusion and loss. Some women I met in a small Baptist-run shelter – really a safe hiding place for a few hours where they can talk to each other and do a bit of sewing before going back out into the unsafe town of Bunia. One woman from Bunia-Kiri stood up and said to us in Swahili: "All we are asking for is peace, so that we can look like you are looking – shiny and healthy. We think that means dignity and you should fight for us to have the dignity that you have, which is a dignity that we deserve."

One of the women I met had made her way to Bunia from Uvira, far south near the Burundi border. She was raw emotionally and angry because she had been raped by the *inter-ahamwe* almost 10 years ago. Her husband and son were murdered in front of her and for a year and three months she was a prisoner of the Hutu extremists, kept as their sex slave. Somehow she ended up at Bunia-Kiri with 12 children, four of whom were fathered by the Hutu militias. Her women friends help, MONUC helps, the churches help, but they cannot help the acute burden of shame and ostracism she feels.

Horrible though the genocide was in Rwanda in 1994 and today in the Darfur region of Sudan, Egeland still calls Congo the worst humanitarian catastrophe in the world. He accused the Security Council of being too slow to act and the mass media of a conspiracy of silence in refusing to cover the crisis.

Recent studies by Physicians for Human Rights and the International Rescue Committee have concluded separately that the conditions of war in the Congo combined with an extremely fragile political and social fabric are the cause of the huge number of deaths among civilians. The chaos and disruption caused by the roaming ragtag bands of poorly trained armed men in militias and the unpaid regular army and police force is what sends so many innocents to their graves.

The studies say that the first killer of all is fear and flight. Desperately poor people are driven from their subsistence farming and tiny villages into even more hostile environments as they seek safety deep in the forests or hidden in the fetid slums of cities and towns to escape the rape and other violence. Typically the few hospitals that may exist are emptied, their meagre supplies looted and their few professional staff forced to run, alongside everyone else. Fields that once fed families lie untended, livestock are killed or stolen. Relatives and friends who depended on each other in the extended family structure become separated.

Dependency and depression are common but unrecognized in the IDP camps. When people do return home to their razed villages, there is more trauma. Everything is gone, the social network that knit lives together is ripped beyond repair. The IRC has conducted four mortality surveys in the Congo in the last five years, despite the dangerous environment. They estimate 31,000 deaths a month from causes connected to the conflict, mostly in Eastern Congo and most of them from disease which is 80 percent higher than the average for the rest of sub-Saharan Africa.

Most of the deaths are due to illnesses that are easily preventable and treatable in other parts of Africa and the rest of the world such as malaria, diarrhea, respiratory infections and malnutrition. Just two percent of deaths were directly caused by violence.

"Life is a nightmare for these people," said Patrick Barbier, the chief of mission in Congo for Doctors Without Borders (MSF), in announcing the findings of studies done by its clinics and medical staff. "Militias prey on the girls and women. Militias and soldiers and police take the people's food and livestock. On top of that they demand weekly taxes. In most areas there is little or no access to health and even if there is a clinic or hospital, people have to pay but there is nothing to pay with."

In Kanyabayonga, near Congo's mountainous border with Rwanda in North Kivu province, the entire population of between 30,000 and 40,000 people was forced to flee in 2005 after Rwandan soldiers and Rwandan-backed militias fought through the town against Congolese troops and militias. Eyewitnesses describe how "men wearing the same uniforms" looted each and every hut, emptied pharmacies and carried away all the food they could find. This is the way soldiers who rarely get paid make ends meet.

It is also the way civilians die in war. They run into the forest and try to live in the thick undergrowth, hiding from the marauding militias. In the case of Kanyabayonga, the villagers stayed away for several weeks. They ate berries, grasses and leaves and what little they could find. More than a thousand children and elderly people died and are buried in the bush. Later the town was re-inhabited, but the desperately poor are even poorer and more war raged around them at the beginning of 2006. According to residents and MSF, combat broke out again on 20 January 2006 and about 25,000 more people ran away to Kanyanbayonga where they sheltered with the original villagers, some two and three families in one tiny hut. Only five litres of water for all purposes was available per person and preventable diseases spread due to the lack of food, water and overcrowding. Eventually the fighting was stopped by MONUC troops who began protecting the thoroughly traumatized and sick people.

The question MONUC, MSF, ACT and other humanitarian agencies ask is: can the people rebuild their lives before the next attack because, although people are hopeful about the election held in late July, few believe the insecurity will end in any immediate time. Therefore, before rebuilding hospitals, clinics, schools, roads and churches, the primary, almost sole, concern of the people is their security. They will come back to their vandalized villages and rebuild, returning to a life of poverty and subsistence, if they can have security from the out-of-control militias and armies.

Church and aid workers tell endless stories of what the fear and insecurity does and why the new Congolese government and the international community must put the security of its people, especially the 80 percent or more who are desperately poor, as their first priority.

Farther north outside Bunia, in the north-eastern corner of Congo, near beautiful Lake Albert, the militias of two tribes, the Hema and the Lendu, financed in part by Uganda and Rwanda, have been waging a sustained war all over the region in order for the client countries to control the riches that lie in the ground for their corporate dealers in Europe – natural resources, including diamonds, gold and coltan. The Hema and Lendu have been ethnic rivals for centuries, fighting over cattle and pastoralist farms, but those were tribal scraps settled among themselves in the traditional way – before AK47s and rich mineral exploiters turned Ituri into a battlefield where tens of thousands have been killed, including ten Bangladeshi peacekeepers whose bodies were horribly mutilated.

International organizations repeatedly warned of the gravity of the situation in Bunia. "What makes these attacks so dangerous," said one NGO worker, "is the way the two groups are now identifying with the Hutu-Tutsi categories that figured in the Rwanda genocide. The Lendu are now thinking of themselves as kin to the Hutu, while the Hema are identifying with the Tutsi. The two groups have competed for control of the land for a long time, but these identifications and the connection they have to genocide have transformed the struggle into something far more devastating." The Lendu, who number some 700,000 in the area, live primarily from their crops while the Hema, about

150,000 people, rely on cattle herding and cultivation for their livelihood. The two ethnic groups share a similar language and have regularly practised intermarriage.

Almost daily, civilians run for their lives. The slowest, the old and the young and the pregnant, fall behind and are killed or raped on the spot. MONUC troops, spread thin, try to separate the fighters, impound their weapons and keep corridors safe for emergency aid and health workers. One IDP camp in a location called Tache was cut off for eight days in 2005 due to the fighting. When relief workers finally got through with supplies they found that 25 people had died. At another camp of about 5,000, Kakwa, near Lake Albert, emergency workers found that two or three people were dying every day, a dangerously high level of mortality. They were dying from diarrhea with dehydration, or normally simple problems with delivering children with no medical help. These kinds of deaths are clearly linked to the war, partly from direct violence but more often from what the violence begets.

No bullet may pierce their scrawny bodies but they are war victims just the same.

Some wars go on killing long after they end. This is the case with DRC. The peace accord ending the war was signed three years ago. The conflict should be over, the people returning to their villages long ago in peace and security. The foreign armies have presumably gone home. There was a peaceful and fair election with MONUC keeping the peace fairly effectively. But the suffering continues at a rate of 1,250 deaths a day. Fighting persists, the army which was supposed to be united and a symbol of security cuts its own murderous swath. The destruction of basic infrastructure by Mobutu's neglect means Congo is plagued by bad sanitation, disease, malnutrition and dislocation. In many ways the country is as broken, volatile and dangerous as ever, which is to say, the worst place on earth if you are not among the tiny corrupt clique of rulers, business people, foreigners and those close to power.

One wonders aloud why the country never makes the news and is so low on the priorities of international donors.

There are various explanations given in the halls of media and donor power outside the Congo. Excuses given with feigned guilty smiles: donor fatigue is one... Congo in its various guises has received billions of dollars in aid that was stolen and squandered by the elites... MONUC and the UN have spent billions on peacekeeping and humanitarian relief... People are tired of Africa's problems... There is competition for dollars between Darfur and Congo and the world is too exhausted – poor world – to take on more problems in another African tragedy.

I listen, eyes glazed over, as the bureaucrats of the aid business offer their excuses and my mind wanders back to 30 July and the two grannies who walked on tired old feet 35 km each way along the rutted paths that pass for roads in DRC. And their hopes for the election were so high. Peace would come now. The world would come and help us now. Life would be good, we were told, if we just voted and made a democracy. They still believed in promises from the rich world and its agencies.

Then I remember a conversation with two Protestant pastors from ECC, one day in Goma. They have stopped believing in the promises from New York and London and Geneva and Paris and Brussels. "You don't send money or aid because you are racists. You come here, look around, take a few pictures and make promises you never keep. We speak French, most of you speak English. Your representatives stay in big hotels and drive big cars and live in expensive houses. No one cares about Congo. We cannot even decide what to do with the little money you give. You tell us what to spend it on, if you dare to give it to us."

I say little. I recall my own personal fury the day after the election. My short wave radio is tuned to the BBC, Radio France International, Deutschewelle for main newscasts (there is no electricity or television in Aru) to hear all the stories about Congo's first free and fair election in 40 years. Nothing. It is preoccupied with the invasion of Lebanon by Israel and diplomacy versus war. More people die in a day in DRC than in all the Lebanon-Israel conflict. I feel personally shattered. More damage and human rights violations have been committed here than anywhere else in the whole world since 1945. I find myself talking with Congolese and cursing the damned system, the empire that decides Lebanon can get millions for a war that will be fixed in a few weeks and Congo gets nothing for generations.

Of course, I am not rational, I don't understand the fine points of balances of power and areas of influence and the two pastors who are called ACT emergency officers are irrational too. We all feel forgotten in the welter of words and resolutions scratching across the ether of our short wave radios and there is no mention of Congo.

The excuses peter out. Reality check. Lebanon is the priority, then maybe Darfur. Watch North Korea, and never trust Iran. Congo? Well, Congo will have to wait, the UN cannot support it forever.

Is there hope? I think not in this anarchic globalized world. Certainly there is no hope if Congo is left to save itself. It is less a country today than a patchwork of disconnected, disjointed cantons. While the war's messy frontlines are gone, trade between East and West barely exists. "It's as if we were two countries," says Dr Pascal Ngoy, health coordinator for the International Relief Committee.

"If you want peace in Africa," says Anneke Van Woudenberg, a senior researcher for the Human Rights Watch, "then you need to deal with the country that is at its heart."

If there is hope, it is the people. But the task is too big alone. The dying continues. Congo provides tragic proof that war and peace look a lot alike. Van Woudenberg says: "We have all concentrated in bringing this country to elections but there has been almost no interest in developing real progress, ending the impunity of people in power, in uniform, and abuses continue. The truth is Congo isn't going to magically become a democracy. It's going to take years of hard work and money."

But will the world see it through? The shame of indifference should be reason enough for action. But without more help to rebuild, without more security, without protection of civilians, and without genuine effort by Congo's leaders,

Africa's broken heart is unlikely to heal. In a decade some-one else may write this story again. The only difference being that millions more may have died.

Chapter Five

Profits of War: Fat Cats Live in Kinshasa

We can have a democracy or we can have great wealth concentrated in the hands of a few. We cannot have both.

(William Sloane Coffin)

As Congolese waited for the election results with mingled hopes and fears that stability would be the result, international corporations who make money from working in war zones, especially those interested in natural resources, were lining up to make multi-million dollar deals with the new government, with their eyes fixed on eastern Congo and Katanga. The mining industry, notorious all over the world for being easy violators of state regulations and exploiters of fragile governance, is especially anxious to continue extracting the rich mineral resources – the richest in Africa by far – of the DRC.

History seems to be repeating itself, as it has all through Congo's existence since the 15th century. And mining companies are deeply involved in the mire. Even before he overthrew Mobutu, Laurent Kabila was signing contracts in 1996 with De Beers and American Mineral Fields worth US$3 billion.

The Times of London reported on 22 April, 1997, just days before Kabila's final victory, that "mining multinationals have signed multi-billion dollar deals for mineral rights with Laurent Kabila, Zaire's rebel leader, to get ahead in what is being billed as the 'second scramble for Africa'. Executives with the companies said they are happy to do business with rebels, who control all of Zaire's mineral resources, because they do not ask for bribes. The fact that capitalists can do business with Maoists and Marxists in an environment so unstable does not deter these stout-hearted businessmen."

In the same story, Vancouver's Kenneth MacLeod, president of International Panorama Resource Corporation, made the connections between war and business opportunities explicit: "We are going to capitalize on the current strife by increasing our presence and our land-holdings in the country [Zaire]."

In May 1997 Kabila's travelling consortium of businessmen and revolutionaries seized and won Kinshasa after a lightning march of 2,000 km from their bases in the east. The state was in collapse after Mobutu's kleptocracy. It needed money as much as a new name. With all the multi-national deals signed en route by Kabila, the necessary capital was on hand to ensure the success of joint African ventures. The names are legend in the tight-knit mining world: Consolidated Eurocan Ventures wanted a reserve of copper and cobalt in Katanga (Tenke Fugurume) with the highest quality ore in the world; Barrick Gold, of Canada, second only to South Africa's Anglo-American in gold extraction, was interested in deposits at Kilo Moto; Banro Resources, also Canadian, acquired Sominki *(Societé minière du Kivu)* whose deposits were rich in gold and coltan, fast becoming the most prized mineral in the world; and the biggest of all, American Mineral Fields, signed three agreements for copper and cobalt, zinc and diamonds.

It was these deals and many others, all with cash advances, that were going to finance the new Congo government's widely acclaimed and ambitious plans for reconstruction, rehabilitation and democracy with multi-party elections in two years. Mining investments would pay the costs but the state would play a central role. The mining sector, for 10 years in disarray due to the almost total collapse of Mobutu's economy, could hardly contain itself. State looting had destroyed the industry. In 1997, Zaire was exporting only 37,000 tonnes of copper (from a high of 500,000 tonnes in the 1980s) and 3,800 tonnes of cobalt (down from 17,000 tonnes).

But DRC politics were taking a nastier turn already. Mzee Kabila's masters in Rwanda and Uganda were demanding too much of him. He played the old Mobutu ethnic cards and forgot about his democratic promises, stirring up the hatred that had emerged during the 1994 Rwandan genocide. The continued and very public presence of Rwandan troops and advisors left him little choice but to fall back on his clansmen from southern Katanga and reject the Banyamulenge who had supported and fought for him, seeking the status Mobutu always denied them. It was a slippery slope the mining companies couldn't stand. So, in an extraordinary decision, Kabila turned on the Rwandans, sought alliances with the genocidal Hutu refugees in the east and denounced Rwanda "as those little Tutsis who will make us their slaves."

Rwanda responded by making its own alliances, the Congolese Rally for Democracy (RCD). Uganda joined the battle and it seemed the roseate bloom surrounding the international resource industry a year earlier was about to fade out completely thanks to ethno-politics. But Kabila was a survivor even though he was driving the country ever further into war and devastation. He quickly pulled in Angola's tough soldiers and troops from Namibia and Zimbabwe to repel the attack on Kinshasa coming from the east. But who was going to pay?

Robert Mugabe, Jose Eduardo dos Santos and Sam Nujoma were not just helping Kabila from motivations of revolutionary solidarity. Not when there were masses of mineral resources to be had almost free. Zimbabwe was granted the two richest reserves of diamonds and Angola and Namibian businesses received similar concessions. Army generals and businessmen sealed multi-million dollar deals to supply food, uniforms and weapons. Vast gifts of land were made by DRC for their support. Contracts on mines and logging companies went to officers and favoured business interests. One company, run by leading members of the ZANU-PF ruling party in Zimbabwe was granted what the NGO, Global Witness, calls the world's largest logging concession by gaining rights to exploit 33 million hectares of hardwood forests, an area 10 times the size of Switzerland. These cannot, international observers say, be considered as criminal activities since the concessions and deals were between corporations and a DRC government desperate for support to defeat the marauding Rwandans who were almost at Kinshasa's gates.

Networks of middlemen, so intricate they were almost impossible to unravel, sprang up during the war years, many based in Lubumbashi, the mining city that sits on the border with Zambia. They were well established and long-standing expatriates in the DRC, with store front businesses where they imported food and consumer goods, but behind the fronts were illicit business interests in diamonds, gold and hard currency trading. Similar networks existed in the east from Goma and Bukavu with Rwanda and further north with Uganda. Perhaps there is no better example of the business of war than that of white Zimbabwean businessman and transport millionaire Billy Ratenbach heading the DRC mining parastatal, Gecamines. These many networks existed in what appears to outsiders a haphazard way, using the chaos of war to feed on the get-rich-quick fever around the first Kabila government.

They were indispensable to Zimbabweans in particular, they spoke English, their local knowledge meant they had access to otherwise unreachable parts of the DRC and they had contacts with the fat cats in Kinshasa. They also had contacts with the large scale interests involved. Ratenbach, with a long record of financial support for ZANU-PF, also scored a near monopoly on transporting supplies to DRC for his company Ridgepointe Overseas Developments.

From the first of the Congolese wars in 1996, multinational mining companies played a central role in the conflict and chaos that followed through to the 1998 war where they were essential elements in fuelling the conflict which reached such intensity. For descriptions of all this we need to turn to the UN experts' findings which trace a pattern of venality involving Americans, Belgians, French, Canadians and Australians in joint ventures with mining and prospecting leases of massive proportions.

On the other side of the 1998 mining war, international mining companies were heavily involved with rebel movements. RCD-Goma fought against Kabila in order to be able to sign mining agreements with foreigners. The de facto separation of the East from the rest of the country in separate zones of control allowed the mineral exploiters from Rwanda and Uganda to pillage gold and diamonds, and for a very profitable period, coltan. Rwanda and Uganda, according to the UN experts, conducted far more of the actual mineral exploitation of Congo than did Zimbabwe, Namibia and Angola.

Western companies have bought the minerals exported by these countries with nothing returning to Eastern Congo except, war, disease, violence, death and devastation. The fat cats of Kinshasa also benefited hugely.

These two countries, Uganda and Rwanda, with few natural resources of their own, started to export large quantities of gold, cobalt and for a while, coltan. The monitoring programmes of the IMF and World Bank never questioned the large exports of minerals heretofore unknown in these countries, even though the UN advised them of the contraband. "Notes were exchanged between World Bank staff clearly showing that the Bank was informed about a significant increase in gold and diamond exports from a country that produces very little of these minerals or exports quantities of gold that it could not produce," the UN reported in 2001.

The majority of companies that imported Congo's minerals through Rwanda were European, mainly in Belgium, Germany and the Netherlands.

By the time Rwanda and Uganda parted company in 1999 and fought each other in the north and east of the Congo, the region was further divided by rebel groups supported from Kigali and Kampala. These included the man, Jean-Pierre Bemba, described at the time as a cell phone entrepreneur whose *Mouvement de Libération Congolais* (MLC), supported by Uganda, was based in Mobutu's favourite haunt, Gbadolite. RCD Goma *(Rassemblement Congolais pour la Democratie)* was backed by Rwanda and at one time controlled the whole of eastern Congo, northern Katanga and parts of central Congo. There was also RCD Bunia, led by former professor Ernest Wamba da Wamba and supported by Ugandans, which controlled northeastern Congo. In fact, Kinshasa controlled little more than itself.

The Lusaka Accords were meant to end this, but basically allowed for a time of rearmament and regrouping and then fighting resumed and led to further expansion of territories. Rwanda maintained that its interest was only a desire to rid eastern Congo of the *interahamwe* militias, but it also continued to export coltan and gold.

The wars of Congo were not just the writhings of a so-called failed state. The war was sustained by regional and international business and the African governments involved in the conflicts. These wars stemmed not just from the desires of neighbouring governments to control Congo's immense resources after the collapse of Mobutu's kleptocracy, they were also tied to the restructuring of global capitalism. Mobutu's form of state control was replaced by another form in Laurent Kabila.

Between the two they unravelled the country and prepared it for war and partition. In many ways it has already taken place and the elections could well exacerbate this. The east remains saturated with rebels, mercenaries, foreign countries and western mineral interests and Joseph Kabila is popular there. Bemba's strongholds in the north and west and Kinshasa leave a frighteningly divided country with only MONUC's fragile mandate to keep any form of peace.

While most international governments acknowledge, as a result of the UN panel of experts' reports, that resource exploitation played a central role in exacerbating and prolonging the conflict in the DRC, few efforts were made to deal with the issue. The DRC example of conflict and resources raised broader questions of corporate accountability in the developing world, particularly in conflict zones where the exploitation of natural resources could help fund military operations and fuel war.

The Security Council first expressed concern about the link between conflict and natural resources in the DRC in June 2000 when it appointed an independent panel of experts to research and analyze the matter. The panel produced a series of reports, the last in October 2003, that detailed how the exploitation of resources had funded many of the different armed groups (local and foreign) fighting in eastern DRC, enriching individual officers of the Angolan, Namibian, Rwandan, Ugandan and Zimbabwean armies that intervened in the conflict, as well as elite Congolese actors.

The UN panel not only documented the link between resource exploitation and conflict in the region, but also considered the connection between the exploitation of resources and international business. The minerals and other resources from Congo were predominantly destined for multinational companies based in Europe and North America. In an unprecedented step, its October 2002 report listed 29 companies and 54 individuals against whom it recommended the Security Council impose financial restrictions and travel bans and included a list of 85 other companies, which it declared to be in violation of the OECD Guidelines for Multinational Enterprises.

The result, to say the least, created considerable controversy. Some governments criticized the panel for basing its allegations on evidence that was not always solid or well-explained. Numerous corporations responded to the report with swift denials and lobbied governments to ensure their names were removed from the panel's lists. The outcome of this severe pressure from coalitions of government and resource-based corporations was considerable watering-down of the experts' findings.

Despite the protestations of complicit governments, especially Zimbabwe and Namibia, and the named companies, the experts' reports contributed to a growing consensus amongst Security Council members and other international actors that resource exploitation was the key factor in the DRC war. The council passed four presidential statements and two resolutions drawing attention to the natural resource exploitation in the DRC and its link with the conflict. In Resolution 1457 the council strongly condemned the illegal exploitation of natural resources in the DRC, noted its concern that this plunder fuelled the conflict, and demanded that all states act immediately to end these illegal activities.

But the international community again failed. The expectation that member states would hold to account those companies that were responsible for misconduct was misplaced. After their final report in 2003, the mandate of the panel was ended and the information uncovered was archived for 25 years. The failure of the UN to follow up on the panel's recommendations has been a major blow to further progress on the critical issue of the link between conflict and natural resources in the DRC and beyond.

The panel's findings sat uncomfortably with Security Council members who were reluctant to sanction companies based in their own countries. In the end the Security Council took no effective action to deal with the role of international companies in the devastating Congo wars.

With the exception of Belgium and the UK, no other member state launched investigations into any of the companies mentioned by the UN experts. Governments repeatedly blamed the panel for failing to forward the relevant evidence to them and claimed they could carry out no fact-finding investigations of their own, despite provisions for such activity under the implementing rules of the guidelines. NGO consortiums in the UK, Belgium, the Netherlands, Austria, the US and Canada filed complaints on specific breaches to the guidelines by companies listed by the panel. Progress by parliamentary committees in Belgium and the UK was found to have been "slow". Civil society groups had been excluded from the complaints procedure.

Following the first report by the UN panel of experts, the Ugandan government established the Porter Commission to look into allegations of Ugandan involvement in illegal exploitation of resources from the DRC. It produced its final report in November 2002. The mandate was narrow and it was only allowed to investigate allegations made by the UN. From the start of its work, the Commission was hampered by lack of funds. General James Kazini, in charge of Ugandan forces in the DRC, blocked the commission from going to Ituri to speak with witnesses and claimed there was no transportation available for commission members. On the basis of its hearings, the Porter Commission report exonerated the Ugandan government and its army of any official involvement in the exploitation but supported the experts' findings that senior Ugandan army officers had "lied to protect themselves". It singled out General Kazini for having "shamed the name of Uganda" and recommended disciplinary action against him. It also recommended further criminal investigations into Salim Saleh, the brother of President Museveni, who had violated the Ugandan Companies Act.

To date no judicial action has been taken against either of these two senior officers mentioned above.

Although the Ugandan army withdrew its forces from northeastern DRC in May 2003, it continued to provide support to armed groups in the DRC. A confidential supplement from the UN panel of experts stated direct transfers of funds were made from the Ugandan Office of the Presidency to support armed groups in Ituri and further claimed arms and military supplies were provided to these groups on a coordinated, institutional basis. In a move to continue to protect his allies, Museveni wrote on August 26, 2004 to the UN Secretary General Kofi Annan requesting provisional immunity from prosecution for Ituri armed group leaders and the suspension of investigations by the International Criminal Court.

The UN panel of experts reported in 2001: "The illegal exploitation of gold in the Democratic Republic of the Congo brought a significant improvement in the balance of payments of Uganda. This in turn gave multilateral donors, especially the IMF, which was monitoring the Ugandan treasury situation, more confidence in the Ugandan economy."

Rwanda's response to both reports of the panel – which accused it of organized massive scale looting through a centralized apparatus in the armed forces known as the 'Congo desk' – was that they lacked credibility and were "biased, subjective and not based on credible evidence". The Rwandan Government also called the report a "deliberate effort to tarnish Rwanda's image, while denying it the opportunity to defend itself."

In October 2003, Foreign Minister Charles Murigande pledged that his government would set up a commission of inquiry to investigate two cases of illegal exploitation of DRC resources by Rwandan companies and individuals. There have been no known results published.

Meanwhile, numerous witnesses and a confidential supplement to the UN report stated that Rwanda continued to help the UPC in Ituri with advice, military training and ammunition. A former UPC spokesperson informed a Human Rights Watch researcher in February 2004: "It is not a secret that we were supported by the Rwandans," adding, "everyone is interested in our gold."

The interim DRC government of Joseph Kabila initially suspended a number of government ministers and advisors who were named as having been involved in the illegal exploitation. In 2003 Kabila ordered an internal review of the allegations against individuals whom the experts had recommended but the recommendations were never implemented. Many of the suspended ministers returned as government advisors.

The accords between the main Congolese rebel groups and the DRC government signed in Sun City, South Africa, in 2002, agreed to a special committee to review the legality of commercial mining contracts signed by all parties during the war and to ensure that contracts were beneficial to the DRC. The committee was authorized to demand compensation from companies for state losses. The national assembly committee took an active role in reviewing a number of contracts and overruling some previous decisions. Its first report was due in early 2005 but the chairman's expressed fear that "powerful and corrupt forces may succeed in shutting it down" were proven correct.

As the historic year of 2006 draws to a close, Congo's longed-for stability is once again attracting international business to Kinshasa for leases and deals in the mineral-rich regions. The London-based Great Lakes Centre for Strategic Studies (GLCSS), while acknowledging that massive insecurity and poor infrastructure are a reality, says that companies which took a calculated gamble during the war years, especially in the lawless and hostile eastern DRC, already have a significant advantage. Junior mining and exploration companies, the traditional risk takers in the sector, are expected to pour into the Congo despite the lack of clarity and the fears of further war.

There is no doubt that the hostility between the East and other resource-rich parts of the country and the capital are a huge worry. Separatist feelings are obvious throughout the east and Kinshasa's hold on licences and leases means the profits stay there. It is high risk investment, says GLCSS, but already lists major players ready to reap the profits of war.

South Africa's giant AngloAmerican Corp. which has operations in more than 60 countries and is the largest gold mining company in the world, also mines platinum, diamonds, coal, base metals, industrial minerals such as coltan and ferrous metals. It has two subsidiaries, AngloGold Ashanti and De Beers, operating again in the DRC and they expect to increase their stakes. AngloGold Ashanti already has a country manager and offices in Kinshasa. It holds a 10,000 sq km concession in the northeast and expects to identify three million ounces of gold by 2009.

Other major mining companies like Australia's BHP Billiton and the UK's Rio Tinto are also already in the DRC. The country is estimated to still have 10 percent of the world's copper, with grades higher than that of Latin America. Congo used to be the world's largest cobalt producer. And its "legal" diamond production has been estimated at around 500,000 carats in the three decades prior to 2001.

Copper and silver multinationals like Anvil Mining, Banro Corp., both Canadian companies, and the British Nikanor, are all spending millions in construction and development projects. Anvil has a poor human rights reputation at its site after being accused of assisting in a massacre by Congolese troops in 2004. Phelps Dodge, the huge American base metals mining company, has taken a majority stake in a copper and cobalt joint venture in Katanga. A South African exploration company, Teal, has plans to produce copper ingots near Lubumbashi and has acquired property for a permanent site.

Australia's Gravity Diamonds now owns 20 percent of one of DRC's largest diamond producers, Mwana Africa, giving it access to a large landholding in the Kasai diamond project.

Deaths and violence around many of DRC's diamond mines are widespread, according to GLCSS, with an average of four miners a week being killed. Militia and gang wars are common and illegal diamond diggers are often shot dead.

Congo's potential wealth attracts a parasitic form of international development that has been called the criminalization for profit of the country. On Christmas day 1999, the Roman Catholic archbishop of Bukavu, the late Emmanuel Kataliko, spoke courageously and publicly. His words, which eventually led to his death, are applicable today:

> Foreign powers, with the collaboration of some of our Congolese brothers, organize war with the resources of our country. These resources, which should be used for our development, for the education of our children, to cure our illnesses, in short so that we can have a more decent human life, serve only to kill us. What is more, our country and our people have become the object of exploitation. All that has value has been pillaged and taken to foreign countries or simply destroyed. Our taxes which should be invested in the community are embezzled... All this money that comes from our labour and is saved in the bank, is directly taken by a small elite that comes from we don't know where... This exploitation is supported by a regime of terror which maintains insecurity... [and] means that some of our compatriots don't hesitate to sell their brothers for a dollar or ten or twenty...

One only has to see the dozens of unmarked jets parked at the country's ramshackle and unregulated airports to know that fly-in and fly-out operations keep their secrets deep in DRC's forests, kept profitable by what the mining companies call self-regulations: no labour, environmental, health or transport laws apply, deals are private, export and import laws are ignored and taxes and customs duties non-existent.

The only Congolese who benefit are the fat cats in Kinshasa, who have thrived there through Leopold, Mobutu, and the two Kabilas.

Chapter six
The Churches:
The Congo Belongs to Us*

We were the unlikeliest lot and that is precisely why God has chosen us.

Desmond Tutu

With more than 50 percent of the Congo's population, some 30 million people, the power and influence of the Roman Catholic cardinals, bishops, priests and religious, both Congolese and expatriate, is huge. Congolese Catholics have also, for many years, played a role as the largest Roman Catholic country in Africa. Much of that role has been behind the scenes, the church keeping a sacred distance between politicians and hierarchy, but when it speaks, it is like thunder and when it chooses to be quiet, its influence is enough to keep policies and action on hold waiting until the bishops make their wishes known.

Its influence kept a wary and watchful eye on the 2006 elections (general and runoff) and did not enthusiastically support the notion of free and fair democratic elections under existing conditions, warning time and again – most recently just nine days before the polls were held on 29 July – that multi-party elections in a country which had only ever held one election, and that in 1960, and which was in a state of violence and destruction, might well prove to be another destabilization of the fragile country.

Even though one of its own, Abbé Apollinaire Malu Malu was head of the Independent Electoral Commission (CEI) and was considered by all, African and international, election observers, to have been utterly independent, competent and above corruption, the National Episcopal Conference (NEC) stated: "At the current time all conditions do not exist to hold really transparent, free and democratic elections."

Archbishop Laurent Monswengo of Kisangani archdiocese, president of the NEC, and known as an astute political observer, demanded that all 33 presidential candidates

*The title of a pastoral letter from the Roman Catholic National Episcopal Conference of the DRC in 2005 which critiques the interim government's corruption, incompetence, lack of concern for the poor and victims of violence and an over-reliance on foreign countries and corporations in the exploitation of the Congo's rich natural resources.

reveal their "true identities, programmes and underlying intentions in seeking power," before the vote.

He spoke for all 47 dioceses and archdioceses in an uncharacteristically trenchant speech on behalf of a church which was criticized by other Christians, including some of its own members, and members of civil society, for taking a back seat in the election process. Suddenly, Monswengo's critics alleged, the church once again wanted to assume almost opposition powers, especially since the Union for Democracy and Social Progress party, headed by one-time prime minister Etienne Tshisekedi, had boycotted the polls. Tshisekedi's opposition party was long a favourite of the Roman Catholic Church during the days when both opposed the Mobutu dictatorship.

Essentially the Catholic leadership, which is by no means united in the political project, fears that the DRC is headed for a dangerous outcome which could continue the war and violence of the past decade. Irrespective of the final winner, their thinking goes, the new leader and the government he heads will remain a divisive force for a large part of the population.

There will be no unity coming via the ballot box in a country where democracy is equated with corruption, before reconstruction of the country's destroyed basic infrastructure, before institutions of governance which have been non-existent for 40 years, are rehabilitated. Many church leaders believe the elections were forced on Congo by the UN and South Africa, and then postponed twice, should have been held when the country was more unified. The inflammatory rhetoric and armed militias and soldiers of both presidential contenders, Joseph Kabila and Jean-Pierre Bemba, are forces of division, controlling their own armed militias and vast areas of the Congo, many of which bitterly oppose the Kinshasa political elite.

The results of the first round prove this, Bishop Dieudonné Uringi of the highly conflicted Bunia diocese in the centre of Ituri province told me over a long conversation:

"Ethnic violence has already broken out even in my own diocese between rival tribes and factions exploited by

Rwanda and Uganda and neither presidential candidate has enough support throughout the country to establish stability by themselves. Without sustained pressure, international pressure and the on-going presence of MONUC, there is little hope for peace. Churches as defenders of peace from around the world must come together as part of that pressure for peace," the handsome, young 48-year-old bishop said.

He had just concluded his first year as bishop of Bunia during some of its worst violence and killings. He was only two years old when the last election was held in Congo, "and look what a terrible result that had for our country. Lumumba was not wanted so your Western politicians ended his rule."

"It is strange to us and our people, who are unfamiliar with your model of democracy which has been imposed on us, to decide that someone wins by one vote. The winner takes all even if he gets 50 votes and the other one gets 49. Whatever the outcome, the new leader will remain unpopular with possibly 49 percent of the population, a very dangerous outcome for us and an invitation to return to the politics of armed struggle."

The first round of voting confirmed Uringi's fears when Kabila won 45 percent of the vote, mainly from the populous and potentially wealthy four eastern provinces who, like him, are Swahili-speaking. His upbringing in Tanzania and fluency in English and Swahili lead people from the north and west who speak the dominant Lengala and official French to allege he is not a real Congolese and therefore ineligible. As a general in both his father's guerilla army and the national forces he is seen in Kinshasa and elsewhere as a militarist and novice with no experience at governance.

Bemba, on the other hand, an alleged war criminal, a millionaire who made his money as part of the Mobutu dictatorship, is fluent in the Congolese languages of the north, where he comes from, as well as those of western Congo and Kinshasa where he won most of the vote. In 1998 he established the MLC (Movement for the Liberation of Congo) as a rebel movement backed by Uganda which controlled vast areas of the rich north where he stands accused of committing atrocities. Bemba, one of four vice-presidents in the transitional government, is loathed in the two Kivu provinces and Ituri.

Uringi says one need only to look at the maps to see a country, with such wealth, divided against itself "by a form of democracy we have never seen or practised, led by people who are filled with hate and greed, and with a natural resource wealth that many countries are fighting over us for. I think this was imposed on us by the outside world because the international community did not know what else to do with us. But, I fear it won't work. There must be a way of making this a government of national unity so there are no losers around to rebuild the various factions urged on by foreign countries who want to exploit our resources."

* * *

As interim President, Joseph Kabila, a Protestant and his wife, Ms Lembe di Sita, a Roman Catholic, were urged by political advisors to get married before the 2006 elections and since they already had a five-year-old daughter, church and political leaders deemed it appropriate that they wed before the campaigning got under way in June 2006. The ceremonies were ecumenical and were therefore presided over by both the Catholic Archbishop of Kinshasa, Cardinal Frédéric Etsou Bamungwambi and Mgr Pierre Marini Bodhu – Archbishop and President of the Church of Christ in Congo, the umbrella church established for most Protestant denominations, known within the country simply as "The Protestant Church". But it was the cardinal who decided and gave Kabila the order, even though Marini is also President of the 120-member non-elected Senate of the DRC and ranks third in succession after the president and Speaker of the Parliament.

* * *

Roman Catholic missionaries came to the Kongo Kingdom with the Portuguese explorers in the 15th century and have been there ever since, although during King Leopold's fiefdom, they were discouraged from sending priests and nuns to the country.

Protestant missionaries became active around 1878 when the first Protestant mission was founded among the Kongo people. Early relations with the state were not warm. During the existence of the Congo Free State (1885-1908), some Protestant missionaries witnessed and publicized state and charter company abuses against the population during the rubber- and ivory-gathering genocide. That evidence helped lead to the international outcry that forced King Leopold to cede control of the Congo Free State to Belgium.

Situated outside the governing trinity of colonial state, Catholic Church, and companies, Protestant missions did not enjoy the same degree of official confidence as that accorded their Catholic counterparts. State subsidies for hospitals and schools, for example, were reserved exclusively for Catholic institutions until after World War II.

The colonial state divided up the colony into spiritual franchises, giving each approved mission group its own territory. At independence in 1960, some 46 Protestant missionary groups were at work, the majority of them North American, British or Scandinavian. The missions established a committee to maintain contact and minimize competition among themselves. This evolved into the Church of Christ in the Congo (in French, *l'Eglise du Christ au Congo*, ECC), later under Mobutu, the Church of Christ in Zaire. The Church of Christ developed rules that permitted members of one evangelical congregation to move to and be accepted by another. It also established institutions that served common needs, such as bookstores and missionary guest houses.

Since independence, church leadership and control have been widely and successfully Africanized, though not without conflict. Most mission property was transferred to autonomous churches, and most foreign missionaries work under the supervision of Congolese-run churches.

Protestant churches are valued, as are their Catholic counterparts, not only for the medical and educational and, more recently, emergency services they provide, but also for serving as islands of integrity in a sea of corruption. Explicit recognition of this role came in 1983 when Mobutu sent emissaries to Europe and the United States to encourage increased involvement by foreign mission boards in Zairian institution-building. Not only was a renewed church involvement sought, but churches were asked if they would be willing to station representatives within the major government ministries in order to discourage corruption by state officials. Sensing the threat of co-option, the Protestants officially declined, although they have unofficially tended to be institutionally close to the ruling party even after Mobutu's ouster.

Mobutu publicly stated he did not want to deal with a plethora of churches and would meet only when absolutely essential with the heads of the Roman Catholic and Protestant (e.g. ECC) churches. The Protestants served the state in areas where state-church interests coincided. Both looked askance at the formation of new uncontrolled religious movements and splinter groups. The government's requirement that all religious groups register with the state and post a bond in order to be legally recognized helped limit their development.

Today the ECC federates 62 Protestant denominations, the vast majority of those in the DRC. It is both a church federation and a council of churches, a matter of some concern to denominational leaders who think it should be either one or the other, both for ecclesiastical and ecumenical reasons. The ECC is a member of the World Council of Churches, as are some of its denominations.

The ECC functions as a religious institution, and provides both a central and provincial administration, and a spiritual forum, for the numerous Protestant denominations. Provinces and the national "synod" have executive committees. Its various presidents are called bishops and wear purple robes similar to Anglicans. ECC is said to be "one, universal, holy, and apostolic", but it also insists on maintaining unity in diversity as they see it as being the only system common to the Bible, the primitive church, and African traditions.

* * *

The impact of the Roman Catholic Church is difficult to overestimate. It has been called by historians "Congo's only truly national institution". Besides involving over half the population in its religious services, its schools have educated more than 60 percent of the nation's primary school students and more than 40 percent of its secondary students. The church owns and manages an extensive network of hospitals, schools, and clinics, as well as economic enterprises, including farms, ranches, stores, and artisans' shops.

As Joseph Cardinal Malula, who was for many years the head of the church in the Zaire era, put it, "For our people, the Church was the State, and the State was the Church." However, despite these glowing words, the church's reversal of its role in relation to the state was striking. Formerly a reliable ally, it increasingly became the state's most severe institutional critic. Overt conflict first erupted in 1971 when the state, as part of its efforts to centralize and extend its authority, nationalized the country's three universities. State attempts to implant sections of the ruling party's youth movement, *Jeunesse du Mouvement Populaire de la Révolution* (JMPR) in Catholic seminaries were strongly resisted. The conflict intensified in 1972 when, as part of the authenticity campaign, all Zairians were ordered to drop their Christian baptismal names and adopt African ones. Malula protested the decision and told his bishops to ignore it. The regime retaliated by forcing the cardinal into exile for three months and by seizing his residence and converting it into the JMPR headquarters. In addition, the state banned all religious publications and youth groups.

Following a brief thaw in 1973 and early 1974, during which the cardinal was permitted to return from exile, relations between church and state continued to deteriorate. The state declared that Christmas would no longer be a Zairean holiday, banned religious instruction from the schools, and ordered crucifixes and pictures of the pope removed from schools, hospitals, and public buildings, to be replaced by pictures of Mobutu. The president was characterized by the regime as a new messiah, and the state took over direct control of the nation's schools. Courses in Mobutuism supplanted courses in religious instruction. Students in the former church schools found themselves participating in daily rallies led by JMPR members, during which they were obliged to chant *"Mobutu awa, Mobutu kuna, Mobutu partout"* (Mobutu here, Mobutu there, Mobutu everywhere).

The tables turned again in late 1975 as the effects of Zaireanization and the fall in copper prices resulted in a progressively worsening economy. As living standards fell, more and more state officials exploited their positions to steal from the citizenry. Catholic clergy issued public denunciations of this corruption. Increasingly pointed pastoral letters denouncing state corruption were published.

The state's takeover of the education system was a disaster and in 1976 religious institutions resumed responsibility for church schools and religion was once again integrated into the curriculum.

Tensions remained high throughout the 1980s and into the 1990s. The bishops' episcopal letter of June 1981, for example, castigated the regime for corruption, brutality, mismanagement, and lack of respect for human dignity. An angry Mobutu retaliated by warning the Catholic hierarchy to stay out of politics. Attacks were launched against several highly placed Catholic clerics.

Tensions would have been still greater but for divisions within the church and for the ambiguity of the church's role relative to the state. Conflict within the church existed between the lower clergy, who are in day-to-day contact with the population, and the higher clergy; the former argued for a more radical structural critique of the regime, while the latter prevailed in arguing for a more limited, moral criticism. Many bishops wished to protect the church's institutional position and to avoid the retaliation that a more militant attack on the state could well provoke.

Too sharp a structural critique could also expose vulner-abilities in the church's position. High church officials enjoyed many of the economic and social privileges of other prominent Zairians, privileges that could easily be called into question. In addition, the church continued to depend on grants from foreign sources; as of 1976, none of Zaire's forty-seven dioceses was financially self-sufficient, a situa-tion of dependency that appears little changed today. The dependence of the largely Africanized church leadership on substantial numbers of expatriate priests, nuns, and broth-ers at lower and middle staff levels was another weakness. Finally, while church officials generally sided with the popu-lace against the government in labour disputes, tax revolts, and individual cases of injustice, they also made common cause with the regime; in its management role in Catholic schools, for example, the church found itself siding with the government against striking underpaid teachers in the early 1980s.

* * *

In some ways, the best-known church outside the Congo is the independent Church of Jesus Christ on Earth by the Prophet Simon Kimbangu (*l'Eglise de Jésus-Christ sur Terre par le Prophète Simon Kimbangu* – EJCSK), an indigenous charismatic movement whose exotic worship and history dates back to the early 1920s. Today its influence is waning in the post-Mobutu years but for most of the dictator's rule, the Kimbanguists were one of only three churches – the others being the Protestant (ECC) and Roman Catholic – officially recognized by the state.

Simon Kimbangu, born in 1889, was already a member of the English Baptist Mission Church when he reportedly first received his visions and divine call to preach the word and heal the sick. Travelling through the lower Congo around 1918, he gained a large following. He preached a doctrine that was in many ways more strict than that of the Protes-tantism from which it evolved. Healing by the laying on of hands; strict observance of the law of Moses; the destruc-tion of fetishes; the repudiation of sorcery, magic, charms, and witches; and the prohibition of polygamy, were all part of his original message

Unfortunately, the extent of his success caused increasing alarm among both church and state authorities. Numerous preachers and sages appeared, many of them professing to be his followers. Some of these preachers and possibly some of Kimbangu's own disciples introduced anti-European elements in their teachings.

In June 1921, the government judged the movement out of control, banned the sect, exiled members to remote rural areas, and arrested Kimbangu, only to have the prophet "miraculously" escape, which further amplified his popular mystique. In September the same year, he voluntarily surrendered to the authorities and was sentenced to death; the sentence was later commuted to life imprisonment, and Kimbangu died in prison in 1950.

His movement, however, did not die with him. It flourished and spread "in exile" in the form of clandestine meetings, often held in remote areas by widely scattered groups. In 1959, on the eve of independence, the Belgians, despairing of stamping out Kimbanguism, gave it legal recognition.

The Kimbanguist Church has been a member of the World Council of Churches since 1969.

Individual congregations are scattered throughout much of the country, but the greatest concentrations have always been in the far western province of Bas-Congo along the cataracts of the Congo River.

Once they were legalized, the Kimbanguists bent over backward to curry favour with the state. The church's leaders, Simon Kimbangu's three sons, regularly exchanged public praise with Mobutu and became one of Zaire's main ideological supports. Structurally, the church organization parallels the administrative division of the state into regions, sub-regions, zones, and collectivities. An insistence on absolute obedience to the leader and a ban on doctrinal disputes also are common to both institutions.

In many ways, the Kimbanguist Church and the Roman Catholic Church exchanged places in their relationship with the state; the former outlaw became a close ally and the former ally an outspoken critic.

IPASC: a story of heroism and faith

The story of the ecumenical *Institut Panafricain de Santé Communautaire* (Panafrican Institute of Community Health – IPASC) is one of faith, courage, commitment and competence in the face of horrific violence and setbacks, which is illustrative of the destruction during the two most recent Congo wars and the ability of an ecumenical faith community to survive and even thrive.

IPASC was my host in the town of Aru for several days, at its third campus in the violent and unstable Ituri region of northeast Congo, close to the Ugandan border. IPASC has worked for 10 years and twice been forced to evacuate its campuses when faculty and students were caught between warring factions.

IPASC, affiliated with the Institute of Tropical Medicine in Liverpool, trains health workers who help communities improve their own health by delivering appropriate prevention programmes in partnership with communities and other organizations. The Teacher Training College has a strong and viable program teaching HIV and AIDS prevention and healing in a non-stigmatized way. Indeed, several members of its teaching faculty openly talk about their own HIV-positive situation. The curriculum also includes programmes on safe motherhood, malaria, natural medicines. IPASC is itself a Christian community accredited to deliver training at diploma and university levels.

First established in 1996 at Nyankunde, southwest of the regional capital of Bunia, IPASC built up a campus, developed a curriculum, collected books, enrolled students and made a huge contribution to the health of communities suffering from all the war-related diseases Congo has become infamous for.

Then the ethnic wars began between the Hema and Lendu tribes, supported, supplied and led by Ugandan and Rwandan troops. Serious fighting began in 1998 but for a while IPASC was untouched despite great anxiety and tensions from the battles raging around them. But, Nyankunde was hit hard in 2001. By the end of 2005 in Ituri province some 500,000 people were displaced and at least 50,000 killed.

For IPASC the years 2000 to 2004 were a time of horror, yet they never wavered when everything they had built was destroyed and a number of their colleagues killed and wounded and thousands of friends and supporters died. Elias Alsidri Assia, senior administrator of IPASC, a Congolese of enormous energy, faith and compassion described to me, in his understated way, the "troubled times…"

2000-2001

"The ethnic war began in our town of Nyankunde in January 2001, and one of the main battles was on the IPASC compound where a rebel camp was situated. The behaviour of the staff and students was exemplary and displayed a team loyalty and initiative, which was outstanding and courageous. Staff and students were evacuated to Bunia until that campus programme was also forced to close because of fighting all around the town.

"The unity within the team was maintained and normal work was resumed within a few weeks. However, the displacement of visiting lecturers from both Nyankunde and Bunia meant unavoidable gaps in the teaching programme, which led to delays in completing the academic year.

"Within IPASC, students were forbidden to engage in tribal riots, instigated by foreigners and militias, and we remained united despite our own tribal differences. We intensified studies of peace and reconciliation and on personal relations and, whenever rumours of conflict occurred we met with the students to study the origins of the rumour, and interpret the possible consequences before deciding on strategies to be taken. Hence a spirit of unity always existed throughout IPASC during the terribly unstable times."

2001-2002

"The second semester of the 2000-2001 academic year was completed and the first semester of 2001-2002 had commenced but the problems of insecurity were always with us. The academic calendar was modified on many occasions, including moving from place to place for teaching and accommodation. At least twice, our campus at Simbilyabo (Bunia) was abandoned because of fighting and IPASC was housed in other church-related institutes in the city, like seminaries and churches.

"We completed 2001-2002 in the midst of severe genocide in Bunia. One of IPASC's students was brutally murdered, half of our Nyankunde diploma students were in hiding in Bunia during the week of their final exams, and the demands on IPASC staff required almost daily innovative planning. The insecurity and destruction of infrastructure in the area halted communications and destroyed utilities…"

2002-2003

"Severe violence and a brutal massacre hit Nyankunde in September 2002, just before the return of students at the beginning of the new academic year. The staff and the few students on the IPASC compound either made their way to Bunia or joined over a thousand people who fled on foot through the dense Ituri rain forest (an area of 65,000 sq km of jungle where pygmies live and hunt) 350 km to Oicha and Beni in North Kivu province, leaving behind all their possessions, which were lost in the subsequent looting. The buildings have since been almost destroyed: roofing, windows and doors removed, leaving only brickwork exposed to the elements. Many buildings were burned.

"Meanwhile the hostilities continued at Bunia with more material losses for IPASC in May 2003. While the buildings at Simbilyabo (Bunia) have not been too seriously damaged, computers and other electronic equipment and radios (our only means of communication) and building materials were stolen. Important documents concerning the institute and its personnel were taken. Staff and students fled in various directions, some following the forest route to Oicha and Beni and some going north. A few stayed in camps for displaced persons in Bunia. With no improvement in the situation, the Bunia team and students were forced to evacuate completely and join their colleagues from Nyankunde in order to save the academic year.

"During the fighting at Bunia and Nyankunde five students were killed along with hundreds of friends, colleagues from other institutes and relatives. We thank God that IPASC's core staff remains intact as they are vital to our heritage and future.

"In October, 2002, the Nyankunde staff displaced in Beni sent three 'pioneers' to Aru to explore the only part of Ituri province where all ethnic groups seemed able to avoid conflict (fewer minerals to fight over) to see if perhaps we could continue to study and work together there. They were warmly welcomed by church and civic leaders who vacated buildings to make room for IPASC. It was not long before they were followed by the rest of the staff and any Nyankunde students who could be located. Offices and classrooms were in a collection of church buildings while students were accommodated in various individual's houses. The activities of the diploma course (from Nyankunde) recommenced in November at Aru.

"The evacuation of staff and students from the various places to which they had fled from both Nyankunde and Bunia proved extremely expensive. The choice was to abandon the two courses at the risk of losing students or to do everything possible to save the academic year and to lay the foundation for the years ahead. In addition to paying for plane trips (road transport being out of the question because of the fighting as well as the appalling road conditions), staff and students lost everything including family and homes and they were left almost entirely without support.

"Not only was the 2002-2003 budget irrelevant, but normal teaching methods had to be modified. To teach severely traumatized students presented new challenges. Teaching methods needed to be interactive to hold the attention of the students, while at the same time, we had to be sensitive to their psychological capacity to carry so much sadness and loss.

"While staff somehow coped with the severe trauma experienced at Nyankunde and their flights through the forest, walking 50 kms every day in the bush, the loss of so much personal and institutional property and particularly of hundreds of friends and family members left everyone, including Bunia colleagues, extremely fragile. Nevertheless, having decided to rebuild again at Aru, they pulled together as a team with unfailing fortitude and courage."

"One of the staff members, Ukima Ukila, IPASC's stores keeper, not an academic, remained with his family near Nyankunde after the main attack. He returned to the campus many times when no-one was looking and took any books he could find scattered around. He hid these in his borrowed home. We were amazed by Ukila's courage as he made many attempts to go back and rescue the remaining belongings of IPASC. After six weeks of regular visits, he had recovered over 1,000 of our library books, and some other valuable documents. Eventually, IPASC staff hired a vehicle to pick up the books from his house. We might not have survived without those precious library books. Nyankunde now has land mines and no one can go near the village or the campus."

The Aru campus in 2006 is still spartan but it is a brand new brick campus with four large teaching facilities, administration and some staff housing. The land was donated by the community and the churches are their support. The trauma is easing. There is laughter and jokes, there are individual stories beyond belief, like that of Ukila.

* * *

The day before the July 30 election, I went with a team of IPASC staff and students to visit an AIDS Club in a town called Arivura about 40 km away from Aru near the Sudan border. It is bigger than Aru, a trading town where truckers come to transport tobacco leaves grown on massive plantations, amidst gross starvation and hunger, by the huge world-wide multinational British American Tobacco (BAT) and exported through southern Sudan. In many parts of Africa, truck drivers are major carriers of HIV. We heard part-way through the tortuous trip that only that day, just before the vote, three rebel groups had signed a ceasefire with MONUC. One of the staff on the trip, Emery Faida, told me his mother, father and sister-in-law had all been killed in the Bunia fighting.

An AIDS Club in conservative rural Africa? Stigma is such a problem for those with the virus that causes AIDS, that keeping the illness hidden is one of the great problems in its treatment. Added to this, there are no ARVs (anti-retroviral drugs) available in DRC except for the "fat cats" in Kinshasa. Most people simply cannot be treated. The area around Aru and Arivura is fortunate in that they are close to Uganda and a hospital in Arua and can get monthly doses of the medication for $10 – if they can get to Arua. No vehicles, poor roads, few bicycles and physically weakened women and men must walk a whole day in the hot sun to make monthly visits for tests and treatment and return with their "blue box" of life-saving drugs for another month's treatment. It is hard. Some miss their essential regular visit and the future becomes grim.

The club is in a small house crammed with people, mostly women and their children. A few men come, one of them – after all this is rural Africa – is president. One of the IPASC students gives a rousing presentation about the trip to Uganda, that it must be regular every 30 days, no matter what, the ARVs (Triomune) must be taken each day at the same time and never, never missed. IPASC is trying to raise money to buy some bicycles for the rugged trip to Arua or, hope against hope, a bus. In this part of Congo the national currency, the Congolese franc, is useless, so people must use the Uganda shilling to buy their drugs. Churches try to help out those who cannot raise the money.

The club gives him rapt attention, laughing, cheering, interrupting with "praise the Lord". Then they talk a lot. There is no stigma here, ideas are shared, support given, children and orphans cared for. And, as at each meeting, newcomers are welcomed and those who have died since the last meeting are remembered. The club even holds parades around the town, identifying themselves as positive and urging those still hidden to come out and force their men to practice safer sex. "We're not ashamed and neither is God ashamed of us, the bad thing is to spread HIV."

I am given translators and the testimonies start: "…when we didn't have the drug, everyone was sick, we just waited to die, it was hopeless, there are more than a hundred orphans being looked after in this club… I couldn't eat, I didn't know what AIDS was, the side effects of the drug were bad and for three months I couldn't work, now three years on, I am strong, I speak out, I even cultivate, and I have time to grow my children… I was a midwife, I knew HIV, I was tested 10 times negative, number 11, came positive… what was wrong with me?… My name is Françoise Ana-vatsia, write that down, I am not ashamed, now my brother and sister are at the club… The club is my family because my real family kicked me out when I was tested positive… People are so afraid of stigma, especially the men, they are such cowards, they are positive but they won't come and they keep spreading the disease… We need a centre here for testing and for drugs, many people are too sick and too tired to walk all day to Arua (Uganda) so they stop, but in the club we remind people, we help them, we walk with them…"

Suddenly everyone crowds into the tin-roofed house. The rain beats down, the deeply rutted roads become rapidly flowing rivers that are impassable. The lightning clips across the sky, the thunder sounds like artillery. We jam into the clubhouse and people talk about the refugees from further south in Ituri where the violence was still raging only a few days earlier. Many of the women say they must change the culture and empower women to make decisions because men like to fight but women like peace and the wars could stop if they began to work together, men and women.

Later, a pastor from the Africa Inland Mission talks straight to me: "I am glad you are here. All you church people and European aid agencies you never come here. To you, Congo is Kinshasa. We think Kinshasa is not Congo, it is a foreign country, it ruins us. They don't know the forest or the rivers or the towns. They are thieves and always have been. We would be better to kick them out and have our own country, those politicians are all thugs, they are to blame for the way our people have to live and die in such terrible sickness and poverty. They keep the money for the ARVs and we have to use Uganda shillings and go to Arua for treatment, not even in our own country.

"This election won't change anything. We want the government to build roads, none of them function now, we want electricity, we need clean water, we have to have peace and infrastructure and stop bribery. The elections are not for us, they are for Kinshasa and the international community. What do we know of democracy here? Less than one year in all our history. We are doing it backwards. Fix the country then have elections. God has blessed this area with rich soil, many valuable minerals, great resources. Why is it like this? Good leaders are like a father who shares the wealth with all his children, but our leaders are all in Kinshasa getting rich and keeping the money and buying big cars. No politicians have come here during the election, we don't count."

Most people in Eastern Congo think the US$500 million spent on the elections by the international community should have been spent on reconstructing the country.

Chapter Seven

Elections: Winners and Losers

"...the business of throwing pebbles into bowls with the most pebbles winning an election, we thought was peculiar. To the Congolese it seems odd that if one man gets 50 votes and the other gets 49, the first one wins altogether and the second one plumb loses."

Leah's gospel, *The Poisonwood Bible*, by Barbara Kingsolver.

By themselves, relatively free multi-party elections do not a democracy make, not by a long shot. The Democratic Republic of the Congo on 30 July and again on 29 October, 2006 (in a presidential runoff) held the first free and fair elections since its independence in 1960. International observers, including the prestigious Carter Center from Atlanta, were fulsome in their praise of the way in which 70 percent or more of Congolese trekked through forests and dreadful roads to cast ballots for president and parliament.

In a country racked by civil war and corruption, not a single death or incidence of violence was recorded. More than 70 percent of people cast ballots for 33 presidential candidates and 9,000 parliamentarians. The ballot papers were huge and the result was a parliament of 500 MPs, the majority of whom support Kabila. The two presidential candidates in the runoff did not distinguish themselves and although Joseph Kabila was elected with a plurality of 2.5 million votes or 58 percent, Jean-Pierre Bemba, with 42 percent, immediately challenged the results announced by the Independent Electoral Commission (IEC) as fraudulent and went to the Supreme Court, which by law was required to certify the results. The courts were set afire by Bemba supporters and the outcome will be debated for a long time...

The worst possible outcome has occurred. While, as the sensitive and experienced South African, European Union and Carter Center election observers agreed that given the circumstances the elections were more free and fair than many in Africa, the country emerges badly split along geographical, ethnic and linguistic lines.

Kinshasa and the north and parts of the west supported the Lingala and French-speaking Bemba with support from elements of the powerful Roman Catholic leadership, including Cardinal Frederic Etsou of Kinshasa.

The mineral rich, Swahili-speaking east, along with parts of the west, gave almost total support to Kabila. The country is split in two and in a precarious and potentially explosive situation. Kabila's coalition controls about half the parliamentary seats and the provincial legislatures remain to be selected.

Most international observers believe Bemba cannot have the decision reversed. The judges were all appointed by Kabila, many of the electoral papers were burned and the 16 percent difference between the two is just too large. The prestigious Carter Center observer team led by former Canadian prime minister Joe Clarke, said that while there were anomalies in the IEC process, they were insufficient to overturn the outcome and that Kabila's victory was "indisputable".

Given Congo's horrific history with governance dating back 130 years, the fact that the election and the runoff were conducted relatively peacefully and honestly in circumstances much less than ideal means that most countries seem willing to accept the new regime.

Yet, although the EU and UN troops managed to keep some control over Kinshasa, where Bemba was strongest by far, after the official announcement of his loss the situation throughout the country remains very tense. Many on all sides of the political spectrum feel it will take at least one, if not two, more elections before things will calm down. It is simply not known if the ill-trained and unpaid police and army can keep the lid on in Kinshasa and dampen the separatist inclinations in the East. Bemba's Movement for the Liberation of Congo (MLC) is split over strategy despite the leader's bellicose threats in refusing to accept the election results. Some opted for a "peaceful opposition". They have 64 seats in Parliament and MLC is clearly the second political force in the DRC. It secured six of the 11 provinces including the capital.

If Kabila's coalition fails to deliver in the coming months and years in terms of peace, rebuilding infrastructure, social renewal and a reduction in corruption, Bemba could gain credibility and be ready to offer people an alternative in five years' time. And to keep him to this line, international pressure can be exerted through threats of prosecution through the International Criminal Court for the atrocities committed by his militias in Ituri during 2002.

But it is not clear. Some of Bemba's allies want a more radical approach. His defeat means that many people to whom he promised lucrative jobs in his administration have lost everything and they are pushing him hard – if that is required – to create havoc and challenge Kabila's victory in any way possible. If they are successful in igniting the fragile capital or bringing in the other opposition parties or if they cannot bring about unity of the armed forces and factions, anger could burst out almost overnight with horrific consequences. Many of Bemba's supporters are resigned or fatalistic to the outcome since they believe Kabila had the support of South Africa and most of the international community. Creating havoc could mean the end of international aid to the Congo.

However, even if he is not challenged in the streets of Kinshasa or the bush in other parts of the sprawling country, Kabila' task is hugely difficult and there are many who voted for him who wonder if he is up to the massive job. Having selected 81-year-old former Marxist, Antoine Gizenga, as prime minister, the leadership lacks the charisma that is Bemba's. Neither is good at communicating a vision for the country and Kabila's record of governance as interim president is not good, which may cause a backlash even in the east and along the borders with Rwanda and Uganda.

The pro-Kabila Alliance for the Presidential Majority (APM) made many promises that mineral contracts signed during the wars and the interim period would be renegotiated. This will upset the greedy mining corporations who want to remain unregulated, but these promises will be constantly paraded before him by the opposition and the foreign NGOs. Nor is it likely that Kabila can fulfill promises on the social front such as ending violence, disease, poverty and rebuilding the shattered infrastructure, given the lack of experience in managing state money and properties. Kabila's future, should Bemba concede, will nevertheless be far from comfortable.

The new president will have to restrain his militaristic instincts and accept the fact that half the country, including the capital, did not support him and resist the temptation to discriminate in favour of the east and against the provinces that voted against him. Failing to do so would undermine the badly needed reconciliation that Congolese need so desperately to rebuild their country.

Elections at a glance

Overall cost: $430 million
Number of registered voters: 24.7 million
Number of voters: 17.9 million, 70 percent
Number of polling centres: 11,000
Number of voting stations: 50,000
Number of presidential candidates: 32
Number of candidates for 500 Parliamentary seats: 9,000
Number of political parties: 200
Last, and only, election: 1960

While the voting days themselves were peaceful, when the first election results were announced by the highly-praised independent electoral commission, violence immediately broke out, killing 23 in Kinshasa and wounding dozens more. In Ituri and the Kivu further violence was held to isolated pockets by the UN's 19,000 troops and a thousand European Union soldiers.

Both candidates maintain professional armies. Joseph Kabila, the interim president, who won 44.8 percent of the votes has a highly-skilled, ruthless and Israeli-trained presidential guard at his personal disposal. Jean-Pierre Bemba, one of the four interim vice-presidents, has a 7,000-member loyal and battle-hardened private army which has close ties to the army in Uganda, which supported him during the civil war.

Ask around the Congo and people shrug cynically in Kinshasa, they've seen all this before with Mobutu and the two unelected Kabilas. In the east there is great anxiety; they have suffered greatly and security is by far their highest priority, ahead even of roads and food and health and education.

The overarching question among all Congolese is this: How are the winners going to handle their victory, and the losers their defeat?

If the new rulers could persuade the people that they are the government, and especially the president, of all Congolese, and not just of those who supported the winners, the elections might be the beginning of a democratic future. If not, the losers will form an alliance of convenience and the country could again descend into violence. More children and women will die and more of Congo's precious resources will line the pockets of the fat cats in Kinshasa. Perhaps most of all the entire central heart of the continent will be destabilized again and again.

Democracy means many things but Congo has had none. The people who voted with such peace and solemnity across the country told me many times that now the elections were done, the country would be safe and peaceful and corruption would end. It was like magic, something they had never had and something sold to their leaders by the United States and the international community.

Elections are only one trapping of a democratic system. Democracy is a system of rights. Without a parliament separate from the executive, a court system free of political and corporate influence, an administration that has a culture that ends the ripping off the country, the thirty percent of Congolese who live on one meal a day and the 80 percent that earn less than a dollar-a-day will continue to live in misery and democracy will be meaningless. With Kabila and Bemba well armed and dozens of militias waiting for their masters in neighbouring countries anxious to exploit the fragile giant, a third Congo war could quickly follow.

However, the biggest problem is the "winner takes all, loser gets nothing" system that has cursed many aspiring – and established – democratic states. Irrespective of who wins, the new leader will remain unpopular, mistrusted and even hated by large sectors of the population he has been elected to serve. The international community, many Congolese fear, will simply wash its hands of the country, having funded and seen through to the bitter end the DRC's first free and fair elections.

Instead the international community, including the African Union and the churches, needs to apply steady pressure on the victor for conciliation and a government of national unity, and ensure that he relinquishes the hope of absolute power. Without this sustained pressure, a peaceful outcome is unlikely.

"Tell me," asked Bishop André Titre, Anglican bishop of Aru, "if you were to become president of DRC, what would be the first action you would take after being sworn in? Would you build roads or restart the health system, train the army to be professional soldiers and not thugs, build schools, order the police to cease being criminals and enforce the law? The new president has to do something." While I demurred, his question illustrates the magnitude of the problems facing Congo.

One of the reasons the international community claims high hopes, of course, is that Congo's immense mineral resources – huge reserves of gold, 30 percent of the world's diamonds, more than 70 percent of coltan for mobile phones and vast deposits of cobalt, copper and bauxite plus the continuing rumours of huge oil deposits – will provide the money for reconstruction and rehabilitation.

But history laughs in its face. From Leopold to Mobutu to Kabila senior and his armed allies and enemies these huge riches have attracted only looters, the people never benefited. So the new leaders will not be overburdened with high expectations.

Erneste, a middle-aged street peddler in Beni told me on the first election day how he thought it would work:

"If the next president gets say, $5 million, he should keep one million for himself, give one million to his ministers and use three million to build roads."

Why not give all the money for the country?

"But my friend, you have to be realistic. That is never going to happen."

And perhaps he is right, for some time, long after this election and maybe the next election too, if there is one. It would be such a massive step forward from the days when Zaire was given huge amounts of foreign aid, in addition to all its mineral wealth sold off to the mining companies with the only tangible results new mansions in Switzerland and a Concorde-size airport in Gbadolite.

Ambassadors from 15 governments devised a structure to help guide Congo's transition to democracy. But they dismissed concerns about corruption and private militias: it would be unproductive, they said, to push too hard for change at such a delicate time. Congo's only well-established opposition party didn't even take part in the election. A non-violent party, Etienne Tshisekedi's Union for Democracy and Social Progress (UDSP) had refrained from playing any part in Congo's war. Because Tshisekedi wasn't a signatory to the final peace accords, he was excluded from a ministerial position in the carve-up that followed, and lacked the access to government resources that allowed other contenders to influence the election process. Efforts by the international community and the Roman Catholic Church to include him came too late. By then the UDSP had already urged its supporters not to register to vote.

Congo has much to learn about the democratic project and very little time in which to do it before the pressures of separation, ethnicity, its neighbours and the rapacious mineral companies force them into the bad old ways of "big men" like Mobutu and Kabila senior. The old bargain between the ruling elites and their former oppressors in the Western governments, plus the corporate world, plus the international financial institutions, plus the aid agencies now in business mode, persists with the new elites, many observers fear.

The predicted betrayal by the new elites is not the entire story. The conventional wisdom – why else would 15 ambassadors draw up the transition? – remains: Congo is the problem, the international community (i.e. the West) is the solution. The Blair Commission on Africa, the 2005 Gleneagles summit and the Geldof-Bono singalongs are just manifestions of the West fulfilling its scared moral obligation to save Africa, and in this particular case to save Congo from itself.

The Western neo-colonizers are up to their necks in all manner of retrograde practices, co-conspirators with the African elites in underdeveloping the continent and nowhere is this more visible than in DRC. The US, France, the UK and Belgium, China and Russia are all among the major providers of small arms and weapons to all parties through surrogates in and around the Congo. As we have already noted, the roots of the DRC's most intractable problem, non-governance, lie in America's thirty-year unconditional support for Mobutu.

But Western governments, international financial institutions and transnational corporations do far more harm than just supporting a tyrannical regime and its successors. Western financial and commercial activities in the Congo are overwhelmingly exploitative and destructive. Research carried out by the well-respected NGO, Africa Action, draws a bead on the startling transfer of wealth to Congo's detriment: "…the wealthy economies of the world are subsidized through a net transfer of wealth in the form of payments for illegitimate debts. More money flows out [of DRC] each year than goes into the country in the form of aid and UN support."

Even if it seems the West is actually investing in Africa, the reality is just the opposite. The continent actually gets only three percent of the world's foreign direct investment. Without exception the fabulous natural resources of Eastern Congo have become a "resource curse". All investment goes to extractive industries – minerals and timber. Capital flowing into DRC should not be labelled as investment, for the people and country get nothing in return except violence and degradation. Foreign companies pay no taxes, increase corruption, pollute the environment, build no lasting infrastructure, pay starvation wages, destabilize communities, become involved in local conflicts and then when their "investment" is exhausted disappear, leaving behind a total disaster. The new scramble for Africa will continue in the DRC regardless of who is running the country from Kinshasa.

Patrick Smith, editor of the influential London-based newsletter, *Africa Confidential*, which has close links to the UK foreign office, calls the new scramble "a system run by an international network of criminals: from the corrupt bankers in London and Geneva who launder the money; the lawyers and accountants in London and Paris who set up the front companies and trusts to collect the bribes or 'commissions'; the contract hungry Western corporate directors who offer the bribes and pocket some for themselves."

And Michela Wrong illustrates in her book, *In the Footsteps of Mr. Kurtz*, the scale of theft carried out by Mobutu (and his successors) suggesting that foreign financial backers must have been well aware that much of the aid and loan monies intended for Zaire were actually destined for his Swiss bank accounts. And the scramble continues.

This is what the new elected democratic government must face on top of a country in which almost every aspect of life has been assaulted and wrecked. It will take more than democracy, regardless of the president and parliamentarians, to cure the Congo's sickness.

These two elections within three months, more than in the combined history of the DRC by its various names, show every sign of turning Congolese politics upside down. Etienne's UDPS, long the only opposition to Mobutu, which it did furiously, is now working equally furiously against Kabila junior, the son of the man who chased Mobutu out of the Congo. Bemba, whose close ties to Mobutu made his family millionaires, is making opportunistic alliances with western factions against the solidly pro-Kabila groups in the east. Many of the 300-odd parties are little more than ciphers for personal ambition, a chance at the mineral trough or ethnic nationalism. The top down election has allowed little space for mature political development.

Getting the elections over and achieving some consensus on the results would be the most positive sign of hope. Consolidating the fragile new and hopefully integrated army is a first step to get the dozens of foreign and national militias out of the bush where they terrorize the local population.

In diplomatic circles anxiety continues about an outbreak of serious fighting especially in the east. MONUC has been investigating during the lacklustre presidential runoff – neither candidate ventured far away from Kinshasa – allegations of ammunition supplies initially intended for the new national army being diverted to Kabila's and Bemba's troops – in about equal numbers.

"As long as the demobilization process of all militia factions is not complete, there will be serious instability," says Daniel Kawata, coordinator of the DRC's national commission for disarmament, demobilization and reintegration, who estimated that at the time of the runoff about 60,000 armed troops still remained to be demobilized. Aldo Ajello, the UN's special envoy for DRC, angrily wonders where the $200 million donated by the international donors for demobilization went. Donor sources in Kinshasa told me most of it had been embezzled before it ever got to the commission. Ajello says there are far too many weapons loose in Kinshasa and in the east and that agreements to keep soldiers in their barracks on both sides of the presidential runoff are not being implemented.

The International Committee of Support for the Transition will disappear shortly after the new president takes office and establishes his government. It was essential in the period between the ceasefire and the elections (2003-2006) and there is no mechanism of future support from the international community in place. Several countries, especially Belgium, believe that reconstruction and rehabilitation of the Congo can only succeed if the new state embarks seriously on a good governance policy, but no one has experience in this. "Let us make no mistake – even with democratically elected institutions, Congo remains one of the most fragile states in the world," a senior diplomat says.

The social climate is also disastrous. Days after the first election, 23 people were killed in Kinshasa in fighting between troops loyal to Kabila and Bemba, similar firefights occurred in the north and east. Schools could not reopen in most cities because teachers were demanding to be paid. Bus and taxi drivers struck in Kinshasa. South Africa has flown in its own Special Forces to guard its diplomats and embassy in Kinshasa.

Large areas of the country were described by MONUC as a "tinderbox" just before 29 October. Despite the highly positive ratings of the international and church monitors for both votes, Congolese are so accustomed to fraud and corruption that many will simply not accept the outcome if it goes against their wishes, and the question facing DRC is: will the winners accept the losers into a unity government for the good of the country and will the losers accept the winners as legitimate governors?

The region is open to serious repercussions too if the winners and losers cannot be brought together in a democratic project. An outbreak of conflict could have destabilizing effects on Congo-Brazzaville and also on the Central Africa Republic to the north, already reflecting tensions from the Darfur insurgency. The Lord's Resistance Army still has bases in northeast Congo from which it has raided Uganda for years through Sudan, where the south is trying to establish a peaceful process. Burundi's new democracy is also suffering growing pains and several mini-coups keep that country on edge. Zambia has had troops on high alert in the bordering Copper Belt ever since the July elections resulted in the violence in Kinshasa. DRC is the heart of Central Africa and violence and instability there will have serious implications for the whole region.

Pessimists call the elections "the vote that nobody won" – because of the huge expense, the massive logistical complexities and the extreme danger that the outcome could impose on the decimated people. Many of these risks could have been reduced had the election schedule and structure been better designed and had the foreign funders – the European Union, United States and United Nations – not been in such a rush. Congo may suffer because neither the US nor the EU is keen to keep spending money after the elections are over. There will be no post-election aid bonanza, rather the fiscal deficit is way over its 2006 projected level.

The transitional government, including rejected politicians, will remain in office for at least five months after the elections, giving them clear incentives to loot the state treasury as fast as they can, especially if they are trying to acquire weapons.

It is enough to make one despair. But, I return to the peaceful, hopeful, proud millions who queued patiently to cast their ballots to choose a leader for the first time in more than 40 years who still, many of them, wait fearfully in the bush and smashed towns of Eastern Congo wondering if the power of the bullet will resume again.

Will the losers accept? Will the victors be magnanimous? Will the thugs in all the countries that surround Congo leave it alone? Will the international mineral interests of the West see a divided, weak, corrupt Congo as a place to pillage further? Will the embattled, preoccupied UN and the international community, continue to concentrate on the Middle East and leave the great heart of Africa the gaping wound that it has been for more than a century?

"Congo is not a stabilized country. But if there is enough mediation, it should be containable," said Pierre Antoine Braid, a Sub-Sahara expert.

Ordinary Congolese tired of years of war and suffering are desperate for peace. "The losers will have to accept the outcome … (they) should just work for the good of the country," said Guy Kabuli, 37, a mechanic from Bunia.

Some observers said the world could not afford to allow Congo to slip back into conflict. "After all the effort and money put in by the international community, if all this fails, Congo may be headed for partition," a Western ambassador said.

Late on the night of July 30, I nestled into bed just north of where some of the worst violence had occurred for years, only eight kilometres from Uganda, the supporter of one of the two key presidential candidates. I listened through the static to my shortwave, battery radio tuned to Focus on Africa from the BBC.

The coverage was heart-warming. DRC was top of program-ming. Pundits were talking of peace and hope, they were actu-ally paying attention to the forgotten giant at the heart of Africa. I heard of big international television crews flown in by helicopter, complete with generators because so much of the Congo has no electricity. It was great, I thought, just like South Africa 12 years earlier.

Of course, it's not over 'til it's over. There were weeks of count-ing by candlelight and long difficult hours to get the results to the electoral commission in Kinshasa. But the people were proud and happy and hopeful. They had voted, almost 25 mil-lion of them.

The next day Israel invaded Lebanon, the big foreign TV crews headed for the Middle East and the Congo immediately dropped to fifth or sixth item and after that nothing. "Why does the world forget us?" Yvonne Booboo asked next morning as we searched the bands for news of the Congo's great achievement. I couldn't attempt to explain to her why Lebanon and Israel were more important – geo-politics was too impersonal that morn-ing. And anyway, the Internet connection was down that morn-ing too, no electricity, no generators for a poor country.

Now there was the presidential runoff coming, perhaps the worst possible outcome. Kabila almost won but not quite and Bemba, a former and potential warlord, controlled Kinshasa and the West. The East was feeling scared and defiant. Had someone stolen another bit of hope? Bukavu voted 98 percent for Kabila but Kinshasa was hugely for Bemba. This is democracy, the ambassadors and the UN tell them, but Yvonne doesn't trust this outcome.

And she may be right. The winner of the runoff will have to deal with the fat cats in Kinshasa and he may join them. His government may sell out again to the international mineral companies. Corruption is so endemic, it is the oil that makes what little of the country works, for Kinshasa anyway.

But that outcome must not be allowed to happen. The world, the international community, must never let the Congo go again. It must be front and centre in the UN and EU and US. No more illegal trade in weapons and minerals across the border, rather, help to the new authorities to prosecute human rights violations, support in the struggle against corruption, proof that the bigger the title, the bigger the right to steal is no longer valid.

The system, I think to myself as the BBC news fell silent on DRC, is the old one imported from the West: winners take all. It doesn't work in the West very well and discontented voters there are demanding proportional representation so that everyone's vote counts, not just the first-past-the-post winners. You can have free and fair elections by Western standards, but you can't have all the power with the winners and nothing for the losers. National unity can't stand that in the Congo.

Everyone who cares, like the international community, the churches – national, global, ecumenical – must urge the victors towards reconciliation, to relinquish the absolute power of this electoral outcome, to ensure a peaceful transition for all Congolese.

Epilogue

The spirit of the Lord is upon me,
because the Lord has anointed me;
he has sent me to bring good news to the humble,
to bind up the broken-hearted,
to proclaim liberty to captives
and release to those in prison;

to proclaim a year of the Lord's favour and a day
of the vengeance of our God;
to comfort all who mourn,
to give them garlands instead of ashes,
oil of gladness instead of mourner's tears,
a garment of splendour for the heavy heart.

They shall be called trees of righteousness,
planted by the Lord for his glory.
Ancient ruins shall be rebuilt
and sites long desolate restored;
they shall repair the ruined cities
and restore what has long lain desolate.

Foreigners shall serve as shepherds of your flocks,
and aliens shall till your land and tend your vines;
but you shall be called priests of the Lord
and be named ministers of our God;
you shall enjoy the wealth of other nations
and be furnished with their riches.

And so, because shame in double measure
and jeers and insults have been my people's lot,
they shall receive in their own land a double measure of wealth,
and everlasting joy shall be theirs.

For I, the Lord, love justice
and hate robbery and wrong-doing;
I will grant them a sure reward
and make an everlasting covenant with them;
their posterity will be renowned among the nations;
and their offspring among the peoples;
all who see them will acknowledge in them
a race whom the Lord has blessed.

To our beloved sisters and brothers of the Congo*

I am writing this letter to you – and to the world – numb with grief and anger, groaning with you in anguish at the senseless devastation of your country and the wanton killings of your beautiful people in the worst wars in Africa's history.

As I ponder these glorious words of the prophet Isaiah (61:1-9) I wonder what can be the purpose or reason of the two recent wars in your country that have been ignored by the West. What must we do which we have not done? What can we say that we have not said a thousand times over for so many years – that all we want is what belongs to all God's people as an inalienable right: a place in the sun in our own beloved Congo.

As we read these words of the Prophet, the words become Kongo, Congo, Zaire, Congo-Kinshasa that Isaiah is describing: ancient ruins... sites long desolate... foreigners and aliens... double measures of jeers and insults... the Lord loves justice and hates robbery and wrong-doing... Oh, God, how long can we go on? How long can we keep appealing for a just ordering of our beautiful and wealthy and ravaged land where all will count simply because we are people, Congolese, created in the image of God. How long will the world ignore us?

This world war, the worst on the globe since 1945, which has been raging since the 1994 genocide in Rwanda, has killed more than 4.1 million Congolese people since 1998 and has been virtually ignored by Western governments, and the western media.

It is regarded, in a racist western analysis, as incomprehensible and shrouded in darkness, the logical consequence of a primitive and post-colonial Africa. I still recall with outrage the racist question the *Economist* posed at the beginning of the millennium, "Does Africa have some inherent character flaw that keeps it backward and incapable of development?" (13 May, 2000). This is used as vindication of the

---

*This is an abbreviated version of the pastoral letter sent by Dr Kobia to the people of the Congo and the member churches in July 2006, shortly before Congo's first election in over 40 years.

war in the Congo by the liberal left who see the only solution to Africa's predicament as their liberation of the continent into the globalized "democratic" ambient of Europe and America.

On Christmas Day, 1999, Archbishop Emmanuel Kataliko, the then Roman Catholic bishop of Bukavu in Eastern Congo, answered these absurd, racist arguments when he spoke about there being no mysteries about the war. He called the fighting a human catastrophe linked to globalization, profit and western manipulation and complicity.

Several days later the archbishop, who was also vice-president of Congo's Episcopal Conference, was deported from his diocese by the rebel group controlling the region and spent seven months in exile in North Kivu. Upon his return to Bukavu he took up his duties but shortly thereafter died of a heart attack while on an official visit to the Vatican in October 2000. He was 68.

His description of the Congo was courageous and honest. The war that has unfolded testifies to his prescience and is now accurately described as "the Great War of Africa".

In a few days (July 30) Congolese are to go to the polls to hold presidential and legislative democratic elections even as the violence and unrest continues. The last election was held in 1960 when the charismatic young Congolese, Patrice Lumumba, was elected and shortly afterwards murdered. The huge country, third largest in Africa with 61 million people, was turned into a dictatorship and became a staunch US ally, used as a springboard for operations against Angola, thereby ensuring constant US support as long as the cold war lasted.

But perhaps we need to understand better and more deeply the origins of Congo's travail and the role of western capitalism in its lifetime of foreign rule. In fact Congolese were victims of the greatest genocide the world has ever known during its colonial (Belgian) period and that history, too, has been virtually erased.

Americans and Europeans are accustomed to thinking of fascism and communism as the twin evils of the 20th century but the century has really been home to three great

totalitarian systems – fascism, communism and colonialism
– the latter practised at its most deadly in Africa. The West
doesn't want to recognize this because they were complicit
in it. Countries that were democratic in Europe conducted
mass murder in Africa – with little or no protest from the
US.

Historians argue convincingly that no country in Africa
today displays the consequences of European colonialism as
harshly as the Congo. After the country achieved independence in 1960, it reeled from one tragic situation to the next:
the CIA-led assassination of Lumumba; the three-decades
long dictatorship and kleptocracy of one his murderers,
Mobuto Sese Seko; and the 1994 genocide in Rwanda that
spilled over into the Congo, to be followed by the first civil
war and the overthrow of Mobutu and then the second great
war.

For some 80 years under King Leopold and the Belgian
colonial administration, Congo was plundered, for the profit
of those overseas. No one should be surprised that this was
followed by more decades of plunder, at the hands of
Mobutu and the multinational corporations he was in league
with. And we should not forget the devastation wrought by
slavery – both indigenous African slavery and the trans-
Atlantic slave trade – for centuries before then. Democracy
is a fragile plant under the best of circumstances, and none
of the Congo's heritage has been fertile soil for it to grow in.

Yet there is an eerie silence surrounding this most deadly
of all wars in the world today and the tragedy of its people.
In February of this year, the UN and humanitarian aid agencies asked the world for US$682 million for the displaced
and hungry and sick. So far, as we write this, they have
received just $94 million or $9.40 per person. By compari-
son, last year's tsunami appeal raised $550 per person.

Ask anyone in places like Kisangani, Bunia, Goma or
Bukavu why seven African armies fought two wars in the
last decade or so, and they will tell you it is a war of plunder,
loot and exploitation. Many of the armies have now gone
home but the suffering of the people continues. War is ever-
present. But even deadlier now are the side effects of war,

the scars left by the brutality that disfigure Congo's society and infrastructure. Plagued by bad sanitation, disease, malnutrition and dislocation, in many ways the country remains broken, volatile and dangerous.

For every violent death in Eastern Congo's war zone, there are 62 non-violent deaths according to *Doctors Without Borders*: treatable diseases like malaria, meningitis, measles, AIDS. Displacement is the first killer of flight. Desperately poor people driven from their subsistence existence into even more hostile environments seek safety deep in the forests of Eastern Congo, forced to run from the amalgam of ragtag militias and rebel insurgencies, many of them former Hutu genocidaires from the 1994 massacres in Rwanda.

There is enormous global competition for Congo's resources, its soil packed with diamonds, gold, copper, cobalt, uranium and tantalum (or coltan as it is known locally, used in cell phones and computers). The waters of the Congo's mighty rivers could power the continent. Its soil is lush and fertile, its tropical forests cover an area larger than Great Britain.

Yet it is this very wealth that Archbishop Kataliko prophesied so accurately was at the heart of Congo's desperation. It is fashionable these days to talk about the "failed state" syndrome of Africa, the process of criminalization and the loss of legitimacy of political institutions. But the Congo belies this thesis. Theorists of the failed state underplay the extent of international business and western influence in the failures they lament. Globalization has sustained the wars in Congo and other African governments played their part.

The two wars of the last decade or so stem not merely from the desire of neighbouring countries to control Congo's minerals. The reasons are tied to the global restructuring of capitalism. The collapse of the Mobutu dictatorship after the global collapse in 1989 of commodity prices led to right-wing American calls for the partition of Congo, dividing off the rich Great Lakes region so that the territory could become saturated with rebels, mercenaries, foreign countries and massive western mineral companies. Is it any wonder that

Congo unravelled, fell into war and, if globalization has its way, faces partition?

In this atmosphere, the world has demanded a democratic election for president and parliament. It is almost as if, by waving some magic wand called western democracy, the Congo is going to be saved, when partition is being forced by politicians playing the game of the western mineral corporations.

If that is the case, then the world must take responsibility to see through what it has demanded. The elections, which the UN says will cost almost $500 million, should be carried out in an atmosphere of national unity and reconciliation, but there is every possibility they could cause even greater division. Outside Kinshasa and a few other centres, there is no national sense of being a country. The East and the rest of the country have virtually no contact with each other. The election dates have been postponed twice. The Roman Catholic Church, which represents about 50 percent of Congo's Christians, is fearful that many of the 33 presidential candidates have not revealed their "true identities, programmes and their underlying intentions in seeking power." All Christian leaders are united in their call for transparency.

The Inter-religious Council of the Democratic Republic of Congo (IRC-DRC) has developed an intensive programme called *Religions for Peace* to try to build trust and confidence between religious leadership. It has established peace and reconciliation committees, undertaken peace-building training and engaged in a project for children impacted by armed conflict. It includes more than a thousand religious leaders.

WCC and its agencies and member churches from Congo, the All Africa Conference of Churches, the Fellowship of Christian Councils and Churches in the Great Lakes and Horn of Africa (FECCLAHA), the Great Lakes Ecumenical Fellowship (GLEF), and ACT International are all pledged to accompanying Congo on its journey towards peace, national unity and reconciliation.

In addressing this message to the people of Congo, I want to assure that war-weary country of our solidarity and

94

prayers, our commitment and action. To the world, we call on it to repent of its conspiracy to exploit the Congo's resources and its people for profit, to end its indifference, and to acknowledge the shame of oppression.

The focus on bringing the country to elections may be laudable and may help end the cycle of violence and despair, but the impunity characterizing human rights abuses of horrendous numbers cannot continue. Is the world that demands these western style democratic elections ready to walk with the Congo and provide the funds and mercy of governments and citizens from all over the globe?

Without money from the developed world to rebuild, without more peacekeepers to protect the innocent, without the genuine commitment of whichever leaders the Congo chooses and without Africa's own leadership empowering the heart of Africa, these elections will not bring any progress and millions of people will have died in vain and millions more will face the same future.

We must not allow the indifference of centuries of oppression and exploitation to continue.

In the name of God, it must stop.

God bless Africa
Guard her children
Guide her leaders
And give her peace for Jesus Christ's sake.
Amen.

Rev. Dr Samuel Kobia,
General Secretary
World Council of Churches
Geneva
July, 2006